gospel[in]life

STUDY GUIDE

ZONDERVAN

Gospel in Life Study Guide
Copyright © 2010 by Redeemer City to City and Redeemer Presbyterian Church

The *Gospel in Life Study Guide* and DVD film script were written and developed by Scott Kauffmann, John Lin, and Sam Shammas from material by Timothy Keller and Redeemer Presbyterian Church.

Requests for information should be addressed to:

Zondervan, *Grand Rapids, Michigan 49530*

ISBN 978-0-310-32891-9

Cover design: Diane Bainbridge and Rob Monacelli
Photography: Marty McAlpine
Interior design: Diane Bainbridge

Printed in the United States of America

12 13 14 15 16 17 18 19 20 /DCI/ 33 32 31 30 29 28 27 26 25 24 23 22 21 20 19 18 17 16 15

gospel in life

STUDY GUIDE

TIMOTHY KELLER

NEW YORK TIMES BESTSELLING AUTHOR

with Sam Shammas and John Lin

ZONDERVAN®

ZONDERVAN.com/
AUTHORTRACKER
follow your favorite authors

Contents

Session 1 City The World That Is

Introduction

gospelⁱⁿlife is an eight-session course on the gospel and how to live it out in all of life—first in our hearts, then in community, and ultimately out into the world.

Session 1 opens the course with the theme of the city, our home now, the world that is. Session 8 closes the course with the theme of the eternal city, our heavenly home, the world that is to come. In between we will look at how the gospel changes our hearts (Sessions 2 and 3), changes our community (Sessions 4 and 5), and changes how we live in the world (Sessions 6 and 7).

How To Use This Guide

This guide includes eight group studies as well as individual *Home Studies*. Each group study consists of:

- A Bible study on the theme of the session.

- A ten-minute DVD presentation by Timothy Keller followed by group discussion questions.

The *Home Studies* introduce the theme of the next session. They are printed on gray pages to distinguish them from the group studies on white pages.

Instructions are in italics and surrounded by these brackets: [ ]

This guide uses the New International Version (NIV) translation of the Bible.

Notes for leaders are located in the back section on pages 148–233.

Bible Study

[*Pray as you begin, asking God to be at work in the group.*]

[*In 586 BC, Jerusalem was destroyed and the elite of Jewish society—the artisans and professionals and leaders—were taken to Babylon by force. The prophet Jeremiah received a word from the Lord and wrote these exiles a letter. Read aloud Jeremiah 29:4–14, and then work through the questions below.*]

1. What specific directions does God give the exiles for relating to the city of Babylon in verses 4–7? How do you think the exiles felt about this?

2. What is the relationship between the "prosper you" of verse 11 and the "prosperity of the city" of verse 7?

3. What was the purpose of the exile, according to verses 11–14? Why do you think these verses were included in the letter?

4. Rodney Stark, a sociologist of religion, writes,

> Christianity served as a revitalization movement that arose in response to the misery, chaos, fear, and brutality of life in the urban Greco-Roman world... Christianity revitalized life in...cities by providing new norms and new kinds of social relationships able to cope with many urgent urban problems. To cities filled with the homeless and impoverished, Christianity offered charity as well as hope. To cities filled with newcomers and strangers, Christianity offered an immediate basis for attachments... To cities torn by violent ethnic strife, Christianity offered a new basis for social solidarity. And to cities faced with epidemics, fires and earthquakes, Christianity offered effective...services.[1]

Is this still true of Christianity today? If not, why not? In what ways does Christianity "revitalize life" in your area?

[*Watch the DVD for Session 1.*]

DVD Notes

[Use this space if you would like to make notes.]

---

[1] Rodney Stark, *The Rise of Christianity* (New York: Harper, 1997), 161.

Discussion Questions

[*Remember a city is defined as "any place of density, diversity and cultural energy."*]

1. Was there anything from the DVD that was new to you, or had an effect on you? Did you hear anything that raised more questions in your mind?

2. J.N. Manokaran, a pastor from India, writes in his book *Christ and Cities*, "Cities should not be seen as monsters...but communities of people with need."[2] How do you view the place in which you live? What emotions come to mind? What do you value about it?

3. We heard in the DVD that,

   In the city you are going to find people that appear spiritually hopeless. You're going to find people of no religion, people of other religions, and people with deeply non-Christian lifestyles, and you're going to discover that many of them are kinder, deeper, and wiser than you. You will also find that many of the poor and the broken are much more open to the gospel of grace and more dedicated to its practical out-working than you are.

   Has this been the case in your own experience or in the experience of people you know? Share examples.

[2] J.N. Manokaran, *Christ and Cities: Transformation of Urban Centres* (India: Mission Educational Books, 2005), 13.

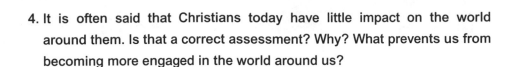

4. It is often said that Christians today have little impact on the world around them. Is that a correct assessment? Why? What prevents us from becoming more engaged in the world around us?

5. The Hebrew word translated "prosper" means "to be healthy, to increase, to have things go well." It means growth in all its dimensions. What types of growth within the Christian community can prosper the places in which we live?

6. In what specific ways can you and your group seek to serve and love your place of residence, rather than resemble it, or remove yourselves from it? What can you and your group do to become genuinely interested in its peace and prosperity?

Session 1 City The World That Is

Additional Reading

See **gospelinlife.com** for recommended resources to help you further explore this topic.

Prayer

As you begin this course, pray that the Holy Spirit will empower you inwardly, that Christ may dwell in your heart, and that you will know the love of Christ and be filled with all God's fullness. Pray also that through this course you may be able to grasp more and more of what it means to live out the gospel in your own life, through your community, and for the benefit of the world.

Thank God for the place where you live. Pray for God's peace and prosperity for it, and that you would have love for it and its inhabitants.

Introduction Of The Home Study

The *Home Studies* on the gray pages are an integral part of gospelinlife. They consist of a series of readings, exercises, and projects that introduce you to the topic of the following session. It will take about an hour to complete the *Home Study.* If you work and pray through these *Home Studies* you will vastly enhance your experience in the course.

To introduce you to Session 2, the *Home Study* consists of a series of readings and exercises that get to the heart of what it means to believe the gospel.

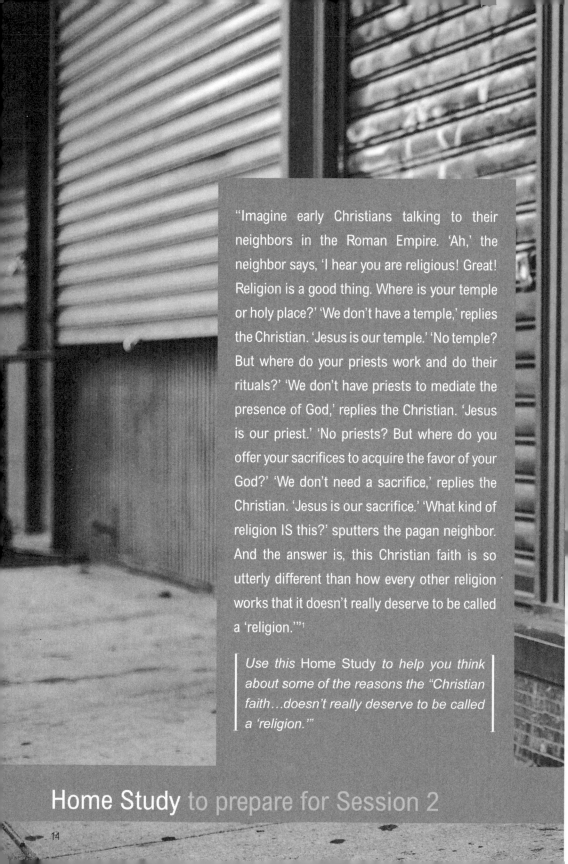

"Imagine early Christians talking to their neighbors in the Roman Empire. 'Ah,' the neighbor says, 'I hear you are religious! Great! Religion is a good thing. Where is your temple or holy place?' 'We don't have a temple,' replies the Christian. 'Jesus is our temple.' 'No temple? But where do your priests work and do their rituals?' 'We don't have priests to mediate the presence of God,' replies the Christian. 'Jesus is our priest.' 'No priests? But where do you offer your sacrifices to acquire the favor of your God?' 'We don't need a sacrifice,' replies the Christian. 'Jesus is our sacrifice.' 'What kind of religion IS this?' sputters the pagan neighbor. And the answer is, this Christian faith is so utterly different than how every other religion works that it doesn't really deserve to be called a 'religion.'"[1]

Use this Home Study *to help you think about some of the reasons the "Christian faith…doesn't really deserve to be called a 'religion.'"*

Home Study to prepare for Session 2

Three ways to live

Jesus said, "I have not come to call the righteous, but sinners" (Matt. 9:13).

People tend to think there are two ways to relate to God—to follow him and do his will or to reject him and do your own thing—but there are also two ways to reject God as Savior. One is the way already mentioned: by rejecting God's law and living as you see fit. The other, however, is by obeying God's law, by being really righteous and really moral, so as to earn your own salvation. It is not enough to simply think there are two ways to relate to God. There are three: religion, irreligion, and the gospel.

In "religion," people may look to God as their helper, teacher, and example, but their moral performance is serving as their savior. Both religious and irreligious people are avoiding God as Savior and Lord. Both are seeking to keep control of their own lives by looking to something besides God as their salvation. Religious legalism/moralism and secular/irreligious relativism are just different strategies of "self-salvation."

Christians may have had both religious phases and irreligious phases in their lives, but through the gospel they have come to see that the reason for both their irreligion and their religion was essentially the same, and essentially wrong. Christians have come to see that their sins as well as their best deeds have equally been ways of avoiding Jesus as Savior. Christianity is not fundamentally an invitation to get more religious. A Christian says, "Though I have often failed to obey the moral law, the deeper problem was why I was trying to obey it! Even my efforts to obey it have just been a way of seeking to be my own savior."

The religious only repent of sins. The irreligious don't repent at all. Christians, however, repent of both their sins and of their self-righteousness.

The differences between irreligion and the gospel are easy to spot. It is often harder to discern the differences between religion and the gospel. Read through the following table which summarizes the differences between religion and the gospel.

---

[1] Illustration is from Dick Lucas, former senior pastor of St. Helen's Church, London.

Religion	Gospel
"I obey; therefore, I'm accepted."	"I'm accepted; therefore, I obey."
Motivation is based on fear and insecurity.	Motivation is based on grateful joy.
I obey God in order to get things from God.	I obey God to get God—to delight in and resemble him.
When circumstances in my life go wrong, I am angry at God or myself, since I believe that anyone who is good deserves a comfortable life.	When circumstances in my life go wrong, I struggle, but I know all my punishment fell on Jesus and that while God may allow this for my training, he will exercise his Fatherly love within my trial.
When I am criticized, I am furious or devastated, because it is critical that I think of myself as a "good person." Threats to that self-image must be destroyed at all costs.	When I am criticized, I struggle, but it is not essential for me to think of myself as a "good person." My identity is not built on my record or my performance but on God's love for me in Christ.
My prayer life consists largely of petition, and it only heats up when I am in a time of need. My main purpose in prayer is control of the environment.	My prayer life consists of generous stretches of praise and adoration. My main purpose is fellowship with God.
My self-view swings between two poles. If and when I am living up to my standards, I feel confident, but then I am prone to be proud and unsympathetic to failing people. If and when I am not living up to standards, I feel humble but not confident—I feel like a failure.	My self-view is not based on my moral achievement. In Christ I am *simul iustus et peccator*—simultaneously sinful and lost, yet accepted in Christ. I am so bad that he had to die for me, and I am so loved that he was glad to die for me. This leads me to deep humility and confidence at the same time.
My identity and self-worth are based mainly on how hard I work, or how moral I am—and so I must look down on those I perceive as lazy or immoral.	My identity and self-worth are centered on the one who died for me. I am saved by sheer grace, so I can't look down on those who believe or practice something different from me. Only by grace am I what I am.

Charles Spurgeon, England's best-known preacher for most of the second half of the nineteenth century, used the following illustration.

> Once upon a time there was a gardener who grew an enormous carrot. He took it to his king and said, "My lord, this is the greatest carrot I've ever grown or ever will grow; therefore, I want to present it to you as a token of my love and respect for you." The king was touched and discerned the man's heart, so as he turned to go, the king said, "Wait! You are clearly a good steward of the earth. I own a plot of land right next to yours. I want to give it to you freely as a gift, so you can garden it all." The gardener was amazed and delighted and went home rejoicing. But there was a nobleman at the king's court who overheard all this, and he said, "My! If that is what you get for a carrot, what if you gave the king something better?" The next day the nobleman came before the king, and he was leading a handsome black stallion. He bowed low and said, "My lord, I breed horses, and this is the greatest horse I've ever bred or ever will; therefore, I want to present it to you as a token of my love and respect for you." But the king discerned his heart and said, "Thank you," and took the horse and simply dismissed him. The nobleman was perplexed, so the king said, "Let me explain. That gardener was giving *me* the carrot, but you were giving *yourself* the horse."[2]

If we give God things in the hope that they will earn us blessings of heaven, then we are really not doing anything for him at all—it's for ourselves. Only an experience of grace changes us so we do good things for goodness' sake, for God's sake.

To become a Christian is, therefore, first to admit the problem: that we have been substituting ourselves for God either by religion (trying to be our own savior by obedience to God's law) or by irreligion (trying to be our own lord by disobedience to God's law). This means we change not so much the amount but the depth of our repentance. We have to "repent," but the repentance that receives Christ is not just being sorry for specific sins. It is not less than that, but it is more. "Saving repentance" is also admitting our effort of self-salvation, our effort at trying to be our own savior.

[2] This illustration is attributed to Charles Spurgeon, British preacher and author (1834–1892).

Paul reminds us of the significance of this very forcefully in Galatians 2:21, "…if righteousness could be gained through the law, Christ died for nothing!" and again in Galatians 5:4, "You who are trying to be justified by law have been alienated from Christ; you have fallen away from grace." We don't just repent of sins, but of the self-righteousness under all we do—not just for law-breaking but also for law-relying.

Second, to become a Christian, we rely on the remedy: asking God to accept us for Jesus' sake and knowing that we are accepted because of his record, not ours. This means we change not so much the amount but the object of our faith. We have to "believe," but the belief that receives Christ is not just subscribing to a set of doctrines about Christ. It is not less than that, but it is more. "Saving faith" is transferring our trust from our own works and record to Christ's work and record.

In Galatians 2:16 Paul further reminds us that, "man is not justified by observing the law, but by faith in Jesus Christ. So we, too, have put our faith in Christ Jesus that we may be justified by faith in Christ and not by observing the law, because by observing the law no one will be justified." In Romans 3:22–24 Paul tells us: "This righteousness from God comes through faith in Jesus Christ to all who believe. There is no difference, for all have sinned and fall short of the glory of God, and are justified freely by his grace through the redemption that came by Christ Jesus." The determining factor in our relationship with God is not our past but Christ's past.

Christians who know the gospel in principle and who have been changed by it nevertheless continually revert to works-righteousness and self-salvation in a myriad of subtle and not so subtle ways. A basic insight of Martin Luther's was that "religion" is the default mode of the human heart. Your computer operates automatically in default mode unless you deliberately tell it to do something else. Luther says that even after you are converted by the gospel, your heart will go back to operating on the religious principle unless you deliberately, repeatedly set it to gospel-mode. This then is the basic cause of our spiritual failures, uncontrolled emotions, conflict, lack of joy, and ministry ineffectiveness.

Home Study to prepare for Session 2

We believe the gospel at one level, but at deeper levels we continue to operate as if we are saved by our works. Luther writes,

> There is not one in a thousand who does not set his confidence upon his works, expecting by them to win God's favor and anticipate His grace; and so they make a fair of them, a thing which God cannot endure, since He has promised His grace freely, and wills that we begin by trusting that grace, and in it perform all works, whatever they may be.[3]

[*Answer the following questions.*]

1. Do you agree that "religion is the default mode of the human heart"? At what specific times or in what circumstances has this been true of your own heart?

2. Look at the table on page 16 and circle anything that is true of your own heart. Is there anything you would like to change?

Calvin, Luther, and Edwards on the gospel

[*Read the following extracts from John Calvin's writings which help to explain the connection between works and righteousness.*]

> I would first ask... Whether a man is deemed righteous for one holy work or two, while in all the other acts of his life is a transgressor of the law? This were, indeed, more than absurd. I would next ask, Whether he is deemed righteous on account of many good works if he is guilty of transgression in some one part? Even this he will not venture to maintain in opposition to the authority of the law, which pronounces, "Cursed be he that confirmeth not all the words of this law to do them," (Deut. 27:26.) I would go still farther and ask, Whether there be any work which may not justly be convicted of impurity or imperfection? How, then, will it appear to that eye before which even the heavens are not clean, and angels are

³ Martin Luther, *A Treatise on Good Works* (Whitefish, Mont.: Kessinger, n.d.), Part XI, 20.

chargeable with folly? (Job 4:18.) Thus he will be forced to confess that no good work exists that is not defiled, both by contrary transgression and also by its own corruption, so that it cannot be honored as righteousness.[4]

We maintain that of whatever kind a man's work may be, he is regarded as righteous before God simply on the ground of gratuitous mercy; because God, without any respect to works, freely adopts him in Christ, by imputing the righteousness of Christ to him as if it were his own. This we call the righteousness of faith, that is when a man, empty and drained of all confidence in works, feels convinced that the only ground of his acceptance with God is a righteousness which is wanting in himself, and is borrowed from Christ. The point on which the world goes astray (for this error has prevailed in almost every age), is in imagining that man, however partially defective he may be, still in some degree merits the favour of God by works… God reconciles us to himself, from regard not to our works but to Christ alone, and by gratuitous adoption makes us his own children instead of children of wrath. So long as God regards our works, he finds no reason why he ought to love us. Wherefore it is necessary that he should bury our sins, impute to us the obedience of Christ which alone can stand his scrutiny, and adopt us as righteous through his merits. This is the clear and uniform doctrine of Scripture, "witnessed," as Paul says, "by the law and the prophets" (Rom. 3:21), and so explained by the gospel that a clearer law cannot be desired.[5]

[*Use the following questions to help you think through the extracts.*]

1. "The point on which the world goes astray…is in imagining that man, however partially defective he may be, still in some degree merits the favor of God by works." Why is attempting to merit the favor of God by works a problem?

   Because it makes us think that our 'works' (and the level in which we accomplish or don't accomplish) defines our place with God

2. In what ways do you attempt to merit the favor of God by works?

   tithing

> *Read the extracts below taken from Martin Luther's* Commentary on Galatians.

As the earth bringeth not forth fruit except it be watered first from above; even so by the righteousness of the law, in doing many things we do nothing, and in fulfilling the law we fulfil it not, except first we are made righteous by the Christian righteousness, which appertaineth nothing to the righteousness of the law... But this righteousness is heavenly, which we have not of ourselves, but receive it from heaven; we work not for it, but by grace it is wrought in us, and is apprehended by faith... Why, do we then nothing? Do we work nothing for the obtaining of this righteousness? I answer, Nothing at all. For this is perfect righteousness, to do nothing, to hear nothing, to know nothing of the law, or of works, but to know and believe this only, that Christ is gone to the Father, and is not now seen; that He sitteth in heaven at the right hand of His Father, not as judge, but...that He is our high priest intreating for us, and reigning over us, and in us, by grace... [6]

Where Christ is truly seen, there must be full and perfect joy in the Lord, with peace of conscience, which thus thinketh: Although I am a sinner by the law, and under condemnation of the law, yet I despair not, yet I die not, because Christ liveth, who is both my righteousness and my everlasting life. In that righteousness and life I have no sin, no fear, no sting of conscience, no care of death. I am indeed a sinner as touching this present life, and the righteousness thereof... But I have another righteousness and life, above this life, which is Christ the Son of God, who knoweth no sin, no death, but is righteousness and life eternal... [7]

He that strayeth from this Christian righteousness, must needs fall into the righteousness of the law; that is to say, when he hath lost Christ, he must fall into the confidence of his own works. But...when I have Christian righteousness reigning in my heart...I do good works, how and wheresoever occasion arise... Whosoever is assuredly persuaded that Christ alone is his righteousness, doth not only cheerfully and gladly work well in his vocation, but also submitteth himself... to all manner of burdens, and to all dangers of the present life, because he knoweth that this is the will of God, and that this obedience pleaseth Him.[8]

[4] John Calvin, *Institutes of the Christian Religion*, A New Translation by Henry Beveridge, Esq. (Edinburgh: Printed for the Calvin Translation Society), taken from *Institute of Practical Bible Education*, The Electronic Public Library. Institutes, Vol.3: Part 18: Chapter 17. [5] John Calvin, *The Necessity of Reforming the Church* in *Theological Treatises*. Edited and translated by J. K. S. Reid. *The Library of Christian Classics* (Louisville: WJKP, 1954), 199. [6] Martin Luther, *Commentary on Galatians*, translated by Erasmus Middleton (Grand Rapids, Mich.: Kregel, 1979), xv. [7] Ibid., xvi. [8] Ibid., xvi–xviii.

[*Use the following questions to help you think through the extracts.*]

1. In your own words, what is Christian righteousness? What is the alternative to Christian righteousness?

to see life beyond this earthly world and focus on eternal life in heaven w/Jesus

2. What is our motivation to do good works?

[*What makes people honest? Or generous? Jonathan Edwards tackled such questions over the years in many of his works. Read the following extracts, which have been abridged and paraphrased by Timothy Keller from Jonathan Edwards' works.*]

There are two kinds of moral behavior: "common virtue" and "true virtue."[9] Let's take one virtue: honesty. The vast majority of people are honest out of fear ("Be honest; it pays!" or "If you are not honest, God will punish you!") or out of pride ("Don't be like those terrible, dishonest people"). Edwards is by no means scornful of this, which he calls "common virtue." Indeed, he believes this is the main way God restrains evil in the world.

Nevertheless, there is a profound tension at the heart of common virtue. If the main reason people are honest is due to fear and pride—what is the main reason people are dishonest? Almost always it is out of fear or pride. In common virtue, you have not done anything to root out the fundamental cause of evil—the radical self-centeredness of the heart. You have restrained the heart's self-centeredness, but not changed it.

Ultimately, moral people who are being moral out of fear and pride are being moral for themselves. They may be kind to others and helpful to the poor at one level, but at the deeper level they are doing it so God will bless them (religious version), or so they can think of themselves as virtuous, charitable persons (irreligious version). They don't do good for God's sake, or for goodness' sake, but for their own sake. Their fundamental self-centeredness is not only intact but nurtured by common virtue. This can erupt in shocking ways and is why so many apparently moral people can fall into great sins. Underneath the seeming unselfishness is great self-centeredness.

Edwards then asks, "What is 'true virtue'?" It is when you are honest not because it profits you or makes you feel better, but because you are smitten with the beauty of the God who is all truth and sincerity and faithfulness. It is when you come to love truth-telling not for your sake, but for God's sake and its own sake. That kind of motivation can only grow in someone deeply touched by God's grace.

True virtue comes when you see Christ dying for you, keeping a promise he made despite the infinite suffering it brought him. On the one hand that destroys pride: he had to do this for us, because we were so lost. On the other hand it also destroys fear: because if he'd do this for us while we were his enemies, then he values us infinitely, and nothing we can do will wear out his love. Consequently, our hearts are not just restrained but changed. Their fundamental orientation is transformed.

> Whatever is done…if the heart is withheld there is nothing really given to God…
> What is given is given to that which the man makes his end in giving. If his end be only himself, then it is given only to himself, and not to God. If his aim be his own honor, then the gift is something offered to his honor; if it be his care or worldly profit, then the gift is to these… If the sincere aim of the heart is not to God, then there is nothing given to God.[10]

[9] Jonathan Edwards tackles the idea of "common virtue" and "true virtue" in his *Miscellanies* and in *Charity and Its Fruits, Concerning the End for Which God Created the World,* and *The Nature of True Virtue.* He also says many relevant things about this in *Religious Affections.* [10] Jonathan Edwards, "Charity and Its Fruits" in *Ethical Writings,* ed. Paul Ramsey (New Haven: Yale, 1989), 179–180.

They whose affection to God is founded first on his profitableness to them, their affection begins at the wrong end: they regard God only for the utmost limit of the stream of divine good, where it touches them, and reaches their interest… But… in a gracious gratitude, men are affected with the attribute of God's goodness and free grace, not only as they are concerned in it, or as it affects their interest, but as…infinitely glorious in itself.[11]

[*Use the following questions to help you think through the extracts.*]

1. What is the difference between "common virtue" and "true virtue"? Why is the difference important?

2. What specific steps could you take to live for God's sake or for goodness' sake, rather than for your own sake?

The gospel and the heart

The gospel is neither religion nor irreligion—it is something else altogether. Religion makes law and moral obedience a means of salvation, while irreligion makes the individual a law to him- or herself. The gospel, however, is that Jesus takes the law of God so seriously that he paid the penalty of disobedience, so we can be saved by sheer grace.

This means that Christians have a unique attitude toward the law of God and moral obedience. On the one hand, we are freed from the moral law as a system of salvation. Our self-regard is no longer tied to our moral performance; we are God's children, loved unconditionally. On the other hand, we know how supremely important the law of God is, since it reveals the nature and heart of God. It reveals the things God loves and hates, the things that are good and evil. Jesus took it so seriously that he made himself completely obedient to it, in our place, and died to pay its penalty, in our place. We can never take God's revealed will in his Word lightly. We can never see obedience as only an option. Instead, we love and delight in the law of God ("For in my inner being I delight in God's law" [Rom. 7:22]), and yet we are completely free from its condemnation ("Therefore, there is now no condemnation for those who are in Christ Jesus." [Rom. 8:1]).

We are justified, made right with God, by faith alone through the work of Christ alone. That is, when we unite with Christ by faith, we are now "righteous in God's sight." Through the gospel we are made holy and perfect in God's eyes.

So, we are made righteous in God's sight, but how do we become actually righteous? In other words, how do we grow more and more into real Christlike character? In theological terms, the question is—what is the relationship of my justification (righteousness before God) to my sanctification (gradual, growing, lived righteousness)? For example, in Christ my bad temper and rash words are pardoned and covered by the work of Christ. They can't bring me into condemnation, but how do I now actually make progress in self-control? How do I become less angry?

In 2 Corinthians 8 and 9, Paul wants the people to give an offering to the poor. But, he doesn't put pressure directly on their will, saying, "I'm an apostle and this is your duty," nor pressure directly on their emotions, telling them stories about how much the poor are suffering and how much more they have than the sufferers. Instead, Paul vividly and unforgettably says, "You know the grace of our Lord Jesus Christ, that though he was rich, yet for your sakes he became poor, so that you through his poverty might become rich" (2 Cor. 8:9).

Paul brings Jesus' salvation into the realm of money and wealth and poverty. He reminds them of the gospel. Paul is saying, "Think of Jesus' costly grace until you are changed into generous people by the gospel in your hearts." So the solution to stinginess is a reorientation to the generosity of Christ in the gospel, where he poured out his wealth for you. Because of the gospel you don't have to worry about money: the cross proves God's care for you and gives you security. Because of the gospel you don't have to envy anyone else's money: Jesus' love and salvation confer on you a remarkable status—one that money cannot give you.

[11] Jonathan Edwards, *Religious Affections*, ed. John E. Smith (New Haven: Yale, 1959), 243, 248.

What makes you a sexually faithful spouse, a generous—not avaricious—person, a good parent and/or child is not just redoubled effort to follow the example of Christ. Rather, it is deepening your understanding of the salvation of Christ and living out of the changes that understanding makes in your heart—the seat of your mind, will, and emotions. Faith in the gospel restructures our motivations, our self-understanding and identity, and our view of the world. It changes our hearts. Behavioral compliance to rules without heart-change will be superficial and fleeting.

In Titus 2:11–15 Paul calls his listeners to "say 'No' to ungodliness and worldly passions" and "to live self-controlled…lives." How does Paul tell them to get this self-control? Remarkably, he says it is the "grace of God that brings salvation," which "teaches us to say 'No' to ungodliness." He explains what he means by the "grace of God" in Titus 3:5: "he saved us, not because of righteous things we had done, but because of his mercy." This is how we say "no" to temptation.

Think of all the ways you can "say 'No'" to ungodliness. You can say, "No—because I'll look bad!" You can say, "No—I'll be excluded from the social circles I want to belong to." You can say, "No—because then God will not bless me." You can say, "No—because I'll hate myself in the morning and have low self-esteem." Virtually all of these motives, however, are really just motives of fear and pride—the very things that also lead to sin. You are just using the same self-centered impulses of the heart to keep you compliant to external rules without really changing the heart itself. Also, you are not really doing anything out of love for God. You are using God to get things—self-esteem, prosperity, social approval—so your deepest joys and hopes rest in those things, not God.

The gospel, if it is really believed, removes neediness—the need to be constantly respected, appreciated, and well regarded; the need to have everything in your life go well; the need to have power over others. All of these great, deep needs continue to control you only because the concept of the glorious God delighting in you with all his being is just that—a concept and nothing more. Our hearts don't believe it, so they operate in default mode. Paul is saying that if you want to really change, you must let the gospel teach you—that is to train, discipline, coach you—over a period of time. You must let the gospel argue with you. You must let the gospel sink down deeply into your heart, until it changes your motivation and views and attitudes.

Richard Lovelace, a professor of church history, notes the following.

> Only a fraction of the present body of professing Christians are solidly appropriating the justifying work of Christ in their lives. Many…have a theoretical commitment to this doctrine, but in their day-to-day existence they rely on their sanctification for justification…drawing their assurance of acceptance with God from their sincerity, their past experience of conversion, their recent religious performance or the relative infrequency of their conscious, willful disobedience. Few know enough to start each day with a thoroughgoing stand upon Luther's platform: you are accepted, looking outward in faith and claiming the wholly alien righteousness of Christ as the only ground for acceptance, relaxing in that quality of trust which will produce increasing sanctification as faith is active in love and gratitude.[12]

[*Answer the following questions.*]

1. What does it mean to rely on our sanctification for our justification?

2. What will it mean for you to let "the gospel teach you"—to let "the gospel sink down deeply into your heart"?

   Life change & transformation of the heart that will alter my attitude and motivation

[12] Richard F. Lovelace, *Dynamics of Spiritual Life: An Evangelical Theology of Renewal* (Downers Grove, Ill.: InterVarsity Press, 1979), 101.

Gospel repentance

Martin Luther set off the Reformation by nailing the "Ninety-five Theses" to the door of Castle Church in Wittenberg, Germany. The very first of the theses stated that "our Lord and Master Jesus Christ...willed that the whole life of believers should be repentance."[13]

On the surface this looks a little bleak. Luther seems to be saying Christians will never make much progress in life. That, of course, wasn't Luther's point at all. He was saying that repentance *is* the way we make progress in the Christian life. Indeed, pervasive, all-of-life-repentance is the best sign that we are growing deeply and rapidly into the character of Jesus.

Religious repentance versus gospel repentance

There are two different ways to go about repentance—religious repentance and gospel repentance. In "religion," the purpose of repentance is basically to keep God happy so he will continue to bless us and answer our prayers. So, in religion we are sorry for sin only because of its consequences. Sin will bring us punishment—and we want to avoid that, so we repent.

The gospel, however, tells us that as Christians sin can't ultimately bring us into condemnation (Rom. 8:1.) Its heinousness is therefore what it does to God: it displeases and dishonors him. Thus in religion, repentance is self-centered; the gospel makes it God-centered. In religion we are mainly sorry for the consequences of sin, but in the gospel we are sorry for the sin itself.

Also, religious repentance can easily turn into an attempt to "atone" for one's sin—in which we convince God (and ourselves) that we are so truly miserable and regretful that we deserve to be forgiven. In the gospel, however, we know that Jesus suffered for our sin. We do not have to make ourselves suffer to merit God's forgiveness. We simply receive the forgiveness earned by Christ.

Moreover, in religion our only hope is to live a life good enough to require God to bless us, so every instance of sin and repentance is therefore traumatic, unnatural, and threatening. Only under great duress do religious people admit they have sinned, because their only hope is their moral goodness.

Home Study to prepare for Session 2

In the gospel the knowledge of our acceptance in Christ makes it easier to admit that we are flawed, because we know we won't be cast off if we confess the true depths of our sinfulness. Our hope is in Christ's righteousness, not our own, so it is not as traumatic to admit our weaknesses and lapses.

Whereas in religion we repent as little as possible, the more we feel accepted and loved in the gospel, the more and more often we will be repenting. Although there is some bitterness in any repentance, in the gospel there is ultimately a sweetness. This creates a thoroughly new dynamic for personal growth. The more we see our own flaws and sins, the more precious, electrifying, and amazing God's grace appears to us. On the other hand, the more aware we are of God's grace and our acceptance in Christ, the more able we are to drop our denials and self-defenses and admit the true dimensions of our sin.

George Whitefield, the eighteenth-century Methodist preacher, wrote on repentance, "God give me a deep humility, a well-guided zeal, a burning love and a single eye, and then let men or devils do their worst!"[14]

Gospel repentance involves deep humility (vs. pride)

Have you looked down on anyone? Have you been too stung by criticism? Have you felt snubbed or ignored? Repent by considering the free grace of Jesus until you sense (a) decreasing disdain, since you are a sinner too, and (b) decreasing pain over criticism, since you value God's love more than human approval. Reflect on God's grace until you experience a deep humility and a grateful, restful joy.

Gospel repentance involves well-guided zeal (vs. anxiety)

Have you avoided people or tasks that you know you should face? Have you been anxious and worried? Have you failed to be circumspect, or have you been rash and impulsive? Repent by considering the free grace of Jesus until there is (a) no cowardly avoidance of hard things, since Jesus faced evil for you, and (b) no anxious or rash behavior, since Jesus' death proves that God cares and watches over you. Reflect on God's grace until you experience calm thoughtfulness and strategic boldness.

---

[13] Martin Luther, "Disputation of Doctor Martin Luther on the Power and Efficacy of Indulgences" (1517), Thesis 1. [14] George Whitefield, quoted in Arnold A. Dallimore, *George Whitefield: The Life and Times of the Great Evangelist of the 18th Century Revival*, 2 vol. (Carlisle, Penn.: Banner of Truth Trust, 1970), 1:140.

Gospel repentance involves burning love (vs. indifference)

Have you spoken or thought unkindly of anyone? Have you been impatient or irritable? Have you been self-absorbed, indifferent, or inattentive to people? Repent by considering the free grace of Jesus until there is (a) no coldness or unkindness, as you think of the sacrificial love of Christ for you, (b) no impatience, as you think of his patience with you, and (c) no indifference, as you think of how God is infinitely attentive to you. Reflect on God's grace until you show warmth and affection.

Gospel repentance involves a "single eye" (i.e., godly motives)

Are you doing what you do for God's glory and the good of others, or are you being driven by your need for approval, love of comfort, need for control, hunger for acclaim and power, or the fear of other people? Repent by considering how the free grace of Jesus provides you with what you are looking for in these other things. Reflect on God's grace until he becomes your joy and delight.

[*Use the above as a basis for reflection and prayer.*]

Additional Reading

See **gospelinlife.com** for recommended resources to help you further explore this topic.

Session 2 Heart Three Ways To Live

Summary Of The Previous Session

[*Pray as you begin, asking God to be at work in the group.*]

[*Read the paragraphs below aloud to summarize the main points of the previous session.*]

Last session we saw that we are not just to seek prosperity and peace in the places where we live, but we are to seek prosperity and peace *for* the places where we live. God says in Jeremiah chapter 29 verse 7, "Seek the peace and prosperity of the city to which I have carried you into exile. Pray to the LORD for it, because if it prospers, you too will prosper." We are to serve and love our place of residence, rather than resemble it, or remove ourselves from it.

We saw that cities were designed to be places of refuge and safety, places of justice, places of culture development, and places of spiritual seeking and finding. So, to seek their peace and prosperity we: serve and love those who need help and protection, bring God's love and justice to bear on a broken world, create and cultivate culture, and hold out Christ as the ultimate satisfaction of people's spiritual search. We are going to look at each of these themes in more detail in the sessions that follow.

This session's theme is the gospel and the heart.

[*Take 3 to 5 minutes to briefly discuss the* Home Study *on pages 14–30. Mention anything you found helpful, new, exciting, or confusing.*]

Bible Study

[*Read aloud Luke 18:9–14 and then work through the questions below.*]

1. **Look at what the Pharisee says about himself in verses 11 and 12. Is the Pharisee a hypocrite? Discuss.**

   Religion defines him, no no heart change as he counts his virtues, it is a statement that is hollow and devoid of love towards God and others

2. **What does the Pharisee understand righteousness to be and how to achieve it?**

3. **The tax collector does not actually say what you see in the English translation of verse 13, "God, have mercy on me, *a* sinner." He uses a definite article in the Greek. He says, "God, have mercy on me, *the* sinner." What can we learn about repentance from the attitude of the tax collector?**

4. Pastor and author John Stott writes,

> 'Justification' is a legal term, borrowed from the law courts. It is the exact opposite
> of 'condemnation'. 'To condemn' is to declare somebody guilty; 'to justify' is to
> declare him…righteous. In the Bible it refers to God's act of unmerited favor by
> which He puts a sinner right with Himself, not only pardoning or acquitting him,
> but accepting him and treating him as righteous.[1]

**Jesus says the tax collector went home "justified" before God. Why? What
does this passage teach us about justification?**

relationship w/God

*[Read aloud Luke 15:11–32 and then **watch the DVD for Session 2**.]*

DVD Notes

[Use this space if you would like to make notes.]

[1] John Stott, *The Message of Galatians* (Chicago: IVP, 1968), 60.

Discussion Questions

1. Was there anything from the DVD that was new to you, or had an effect on you? Did you hear anything that raised more questions in your mind?

2. Which of the two brothers is easiest for you to identify with, and why?

3. What emotions and attitudes does the elder brother display, and what does this show about his relationship with God?

4. What do you think it means "to repent not only of our bad things, but also for the reason we did our good things"?

5. "If I gave you a test on justification by grace alone through faith alone through the substitutionary work of Christ alone, you'd probably get 100 percent." If we're justified by grace alone, not by our good works or our moral efforts or anything we can do, what motivates us to live an obedient, repentant life?

6. If Jesus is our true elder brother, how does it change the way we live on a daily basis?

Prayer

Praise God that he is the Father who loves and pursues both types of sons. Thank him for his initiating love as well as the costly search of the true elder brother, Jesus Christ. Confess the occasions when it is easy to forget that God is like this, and pray that you would live by grace alone. Ask for God's grace to lead you to a repentance that brings new freedom from sin and from self-righteousness, as well as a greater appreciation of God's love and forgiveness.

Introduction Of The Home Study

To introduce you to Session 3, the *Home Study* focuses on the idea of idolatry and gives you a worksheet, a series of questions, and some exercises to help you identify the idols of your own heart.

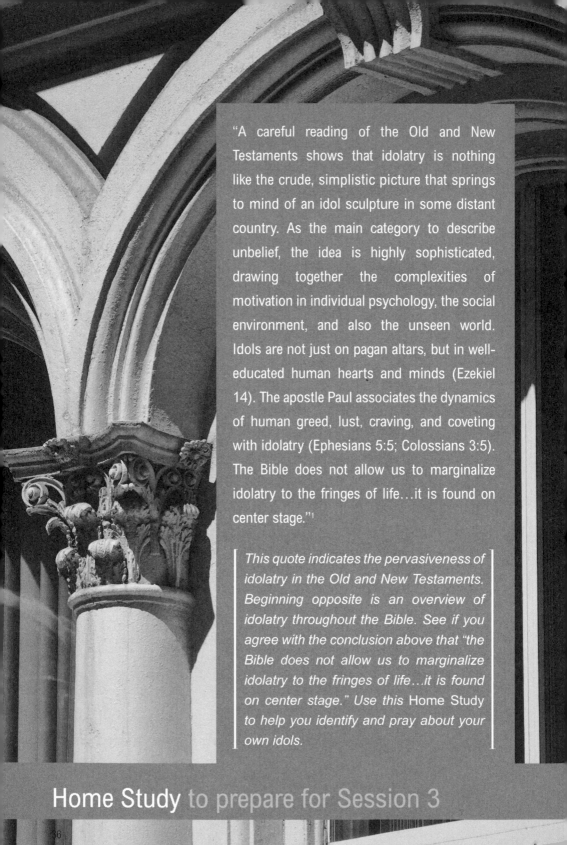

"A careful reading of the Old and New Testaments shows that idolatry is nothing like the crude, simplistic picture that springs to mind of an idol sculpture in some distant country. As the main category to describe unbelief, the idea is highly sophisticated, drawing together the complexities of motivation in individual psychology, the social environment, and also the unseen world. Idols are not just on pagan altars, but in well-educated human hearts and minds (Ezekiel 14). The apostle Paul associates the dynamics of human greed, lust, craving, and coveting with idolatry (Ephesians 5:5; Colossians 3:5). The Bible does not allow us to marginalize idolatry to the fringes of life…it is found on center stage."[1]

This quote indicates the pervasiveness of idolatry in the Old and New Testaments. Beginning opposite is an overview of idolatry throughout the Bible. See if you agree with the conclusion above that "the Bible does not allow us to marginalize idolatry to the fringes of life…it is found on center stage." Use this Home Study *to help you identify and pray about your own idols.*

Home Study to prepare for Session 3

Idolatry in the Old Testament

In the beginning—idolatry

In the beginning, human beings were made to (1) worship and serve God, and then (2) to rule over all created things in God's name (Gen. 1:26–28). Instead, we fell into sin. When Paul sums up the fall of humanity into sin, he does so by describing it in terms of idolatry. He says we refused to give God glory (i.e., to make him the most important thing) and instead chose certain parts of creation to glorify in his stead: "[They] exchanged the glory of the immortal God…and worshiped and served created things rather than the Creator" (Rom. 1:23–25). In short, we reversed the originally intended order. Human beings came to (1) worship and serve created things, and therefore (2) the created things came to rule over them.

The Law—against idols

The great sin of the Mosaic period is the making of a golden calf (Ex. 32). The Ten Commandments' first two and most basic laws are against idolatry. The first commandment prohibits worshiping other gods; the second commandment prohibits worshiping God idolatrously, as we want him to be. After God's code of covenant behavior is given in Exodus 20–23, there is a summary warning against making a covenant with other gods (Ex. 23:24) because they "snare" you (Ex. 23:33). Exodus does not envision any third option. We will either worship God, or we will worship some created thing (an idol). Every human personality, every human community, and every human thought-form will be based on some ultimate concern or some ultimate allegiance to something. Luther put it like this:

> [A]ll those who do not at all times trust God and do not in all their works or sufferings, life and death, trust in His favor, grace and good-will, but seek His favor in other things or in themselves, do not keep this [First] Commandment, and practise real idolatry, even if they were to do the works of all the other Commandments, and in addition had all the prayers, fasting, obedience, patience, chastity, and innocence of all the saints combined. For the chief work is not present, without which all the others are nothing but mere sham, show and pretence.[2]

[1] Richard Keyes, "The Idol Factory" in *No God but God: Breaking with the Idols of Our Age*, ed. Os Guinness and John Seel (Chicago: Moody Press, 1992), 31. [2] Martin Luther, *A Treatise on Good Works* (Whitefish, Mont.: Kessinger, 1520), Part X, 18.

The Psalms—praying against idols

In the Psalms, the prayers of the people are not only toward God, but also against idols. Psalm 24:3–4 says, "Who may ascend the hill of the LORD? Who may stand in his holy place? He who has clean hands and a pure heart, who does not lift up his soul to an idol... "

The Prophets—polemic against idols

Isaiah, Jeremiah, and Ezekiel leveled an enormous polemic against the worship of idols. First, they said, an idol is empty, nothing, powerless. An idol is nothing but what we ourselves have made, the work of our own hands (Isa. 2:8; Jer. 1:16). Thus, an idol is something we make in our image. It is only, in a sense, worshiping ourselves, or a reflection of our own sensibility (Isa. 44:10–13).

Second, an idol is, paradoxically, a spiritually dangerous power that saps you of all power. This is a triple paradox. Idols are powerless things that are all about getting power. The more you seek power through them, however, the more they drain you of strength. Idols bring about terrible spiritual blindness of heart and mind (Isa. 44:9, 18), and the idolater is self-deluded through a web of lies (Isa. 44:20). Also, idols bring about slavery. Jeremiah likens our relationship to idols as a love-addicted person to his or her lover (Jer. 2:25). Idols poison the heart into complete dependence on them (Isa. 44:17); they completely capture our hearts (Ezek. 14:1–5). They become our lord, as author Rebecca Pippert observes.

> Whatever controls us is our lord. The person who seeks power is controlled by power. The person who seeks acceptance is controlled by the people he or she wants to please. We do not control ourselves. We are controlled by the lord of our life.[3]

Idolatry in the New Testament

The word *epithumiai*, meaning "inordinate desires," is very common in the New Testament and has strong links to the idea of idolatry. Every sin is rooted in the inordinate desire for something, which comes because we are

Home Study to prepare for Session 3

trusting in an idol rather than in Christ for our righteousness or salvation. This is why the word *epithumiai* shows up in so many of the New Testament sections that treat Christian character, such as the "fruit of the Spirit" passage (see Gal. 5:22–26). Author and counselor David Powlison explains:

> If "idolatry" is the characteristic and summary Old Testament word for our drift from God, then "desires" (*epithumiai*) is the characteristic and summary New Testament word for the same drift.[4] Both are shorthand for *the* problem of human beings… [T]he New Testament merges the concept of idolatry and the concept of inordinate, life-ruling desires. Idolatry becomes a problem of the heart, a metaphor for human lust, craving, yearning, and greedy demand.[5]

Romans 1:18–25

This passage tells us that the reason we create idols is because we want to control our lives, though we know that we owe God everything. "For although they knew God, they neither glorified him as God nor gave thanks to him" (v. 21). Verse 25 describes the strategy for control: taking created things and setting our hearts on them and building our lives around them. Since we need to worship something because of how we are created, we cannot eliminate God without creating God-substitutes. "They exchanged the truth of God for a lie" (Rom. 1:25).

Galatians 4:8–9

Paul is saying, "Don't go back to idolatry." Paul reminds the Galatians that they had once been enslaved "to those who by nature are not gods. But…how is it that you are turning back to those weak and miserable principles? Do you wish to be enslaved by them all over again?" (Gal. 4:8–9). The danger to the Galatians is following those who are telling them to be circumcised and who are trying to lure them into moralism, thereby clouding their understanding of salvation. Paul talks of this as a return to idolatry. The implications are significant. If anything but Christ is your source of salvation, you are falling into idolatry. Whether you sacrifice to a statue or seek to merit heaven through conscientious morality, you are setting up something besides God as your ultimate hope, and it will enslave you.

---

[3] Rebecca Manley Pippert, *Out of the Saltshaker and into the World* (Downers Grove, Ill.: InterVarsity Press, 1979), 53. [4] "See such summary statements by Paul, Peter, John, and James as Galatians 5:16ff; Ephesians 2:3 and 4:22; 1 Peter 2:11 and 4:2; 1 John 2:16; James 1:14f, where *epithumiai* is the catch-all for what is wrong with us." Footnote taken from the article. [5] David Powlison, "Idols of the Heart and 'Vanity Fair'," *The Journal of Biblical Counseling*, Volume 13, Number 2 (Winter 1995): 36.

1 John 5:21

The last verse of 1 John is, "Dear children, keep yourselves from idols." John has not mentioned idolatry by name once in the entire letter, so we have to conclude one of two things. Either he is now, in the very last sentence, changing the whole subject, or he is summarizing all he has been saying in the epistle about living in the light (holiness), love, and truth. The latter seems more reasonable—and these implications are also significant. John, in one brief statement, is expressing in negative terms what he had spent the whole letter putting in the positive. This must mean that the only way to walk in holiness, love, and truth is to keep free from idols. They are mutually exclusive. Underlying any failure to walk in holiness is some form of idolatry.

Identifying your idols

Why do we lie, or fail to love, or break our promises, or live selfishly? Of course, the general answer is "Because we are weak and sinful," but the specific answer is that there is something besides Jesus Christ that we feel we must have to be happy, something that is more important to our heart than God, something that is enslaving our heart through inordinate desires. The key to change (and even to self-understanding) is therefore to identify the idols of the heart. Theologian and author Thomas Oden writes,

> Every self exists in relation to values perceived as making life worth living. A *value* is anything good in the created order—any idea, relation, object or person in which one has an interest, from which one derives significance… These values compete… In time one is prone to choose a *center of value* by which other values are judged. When a finite value has been elevated to centrality and imagined as a final source of meaning, then one has chosen…a god… One has a god when a finite value is…viewed as that without which one cannot receive life joyfully.[6]

We often don't go deeply enough to analyze our idol-structures. For example, "money" is of course an idol; yet, in another sense, money can be sought to satisfy other very different idols. That is, some people want money in order to control their world and life (such people usually don't spend their money, but save it), while others want money for access to social circles and for making themselves beautiful and attractive (such people do spend their money on themselves). The same goes for sex. Some people use sex in order to get power over others, others in order to feel approved and loved, and others just for pleasure or comfort. Richard Keyes in his essay *The Idol Factory* notes,

> All sorts of things are potential idols... If this is so, how do we determine when something is becoming or has become an idol?... As soon as our loyalty to anything leads us to disobey God, we are in danger of making it an idol... An idol can be a physical object, a property, a person, an activity, a role, an institution, a hope, an image, an idea, a pleasure, a hero...
>
> • Work, a commandment of God, can become an idol if it is pursued so exclusively that responsibilities to one's family are ignored.
> • Family, an institution of God Himself, can become an idol if one is so preoccupied with the family that no one outside of one's own family is cared for.
> • Being well-liked, a perfectly legitimate hope, becomes an idol if the attachment to it means that one never risks disapproval.[7]

[*Answer these questions, which will begin to help you identify your idols.*]

1. What is my greatest nightmare? What do I worry about most?

2. What do I rely on or comfort myself with when things go badly or become difficult?

[6] Thomas C. Oden, *Two Worlds: Notes on the Death of Modernity in America and Russia* (Downers Grove, Ill: InterVarsity Press, 1992), 94–95.
[7] Richard Keyes, "The Idol Factory" in *No God but God: Breaking with the Idols of Our Age*, ed. Os Guinness and John Seel (Chicago: Moody Press, 1992), 32–33.

3. What makes me feel the most self-worth? What am I the proudest of?

4. What do I really want and expect out of life? What would really make me happy?

> *Read through the statements opposite and circle the thoughts that most resonate with you.*

"Life only has meaning/I only have worth if… I have power and influence over others."   (Power idolatry)

"Life only has meaning/I only have worth if… I am loved and respected by _____."   (Approval idolatry)

"Life only has meaning/I only have worth if…
I have this kind of pleasure experience, a particular quality of life."   (Comfort idolatry)

"Life only has meaning/I only have worth if…
I am able to get mastery over my life in the area of _____."   (Control idolatry)

"Life only has meaning/I only have worth if… people are dependent on me and need me."   (Helping idolatry)

"Life only has meaning/I only have worth if…
someone is there to protect me and keep me safe."   (Dependence idolatry)

"Life only has meaning/I only have worth if…
I am completely free from obligations or responsibilities to take care of someone."   (Independence idolatry)

"Life only has meaning/I only have worth if… I am highly productive and getting a lot done."   (Work idolatry)

"Life only has meaning/I only have worth if…
I am being recognized for my accomplishments, and I am excelling in my work."   (Achievement idolatry)

"Life only has meaning/I only have worth if…
I have a certain level of wealth, financial freedom, and very nice possessions."   (Materialism idolatry)

"Life only has meaning/I only have worth if…
I am adhering to my religion's moral codes and accomplished in its activities."   (Religion idolatry)

"Life only has meaning/I only have worth if…
this one person is in my life and happy to be there, and/or happy with me."   (Individual person idolatry)

"Life only has meaning/I only have worth if…
I feel I am totally independent of organized religion and am living by a self-made morality."   (Irreligion idolatry)

"Life only has meaning/I only have worth if…
my race and culture is ascendant and recognized as superior."   (Racial/cultural idolatry)

"Life only has meaning/I only have worth if…
a particular social grouping or professional grouping or other group lets me in."   (Inner ring idolatry)

"Life only has meaning/I only have worth if…
my children and/or my parents are happy and happy with me."   (Family idolatry)

"Life only has meaning/I only have worth if… Mr. or Ms. 'Right' is in love with me."   (Relationship idolatry)

"Life only has meaning/I only have worth if…
I am hurting, in a problem; only then do I feel worthy of love or able to deal with guilt."   (Suffering idolatry)

"Life only has meaning/I only have worth if…
my political or social cause is making progress and ascending in influence or power."   (Ideology idolatry)

"Life only has meaning/I only have worth if… I have a particular kind of look or body image."   (Image idolatry)

If you circled one of the first four on the previous list, the following table may help you think through some of the issues involved.

If you seek	Your greatest nightmare	People around you often feel	Your problem emotion
POWER (Success, winning, influence)	Humiliation	Used	Anger
APPROVAL (Affirmation, love, relationships)	Rejection	Smothered	Cowardice
COMFORT (Privacy, lack of stress, freedom)	Stress, demands	Neglected	Boredom
CONTROL (Self-discipline, certainty, standards)	Uncertainty	Condemned	Worry

Now that you've answered the questions above, look for common themes. What things tend to be too important to you? What are your idols?

Home Study to prepare for Session 3

Displacing your idols

Three approaches to personal change appear below.

The "moralizing" approach

Basic analysis: Your problem is that you are doing wrong. Repent!

This approach focuses on behavior, but doesn't go deeply enough. We must find out the *why* of our behavior. Why do I find I want to do the wrong things? What inordinate desires are drawing me to do so? What are the idols and false beliefs behind them?

Telling someone (or yourself) to "Repent and change your behavior" is insufficient, because you still hold a belief that says, "Even if you live up to moral standards but don't have this particular thing that you treasure, you are still a failure."

You must replace this belief by repenting for the sin beneath it all—your particular idolatry.

The "psychologizing" approach

Basic analysis: Your problem is that you don't see that God loves you as you are. Rejoice!

This approach focuses on feelings, which seem to be "deeper" than behaviors, but it also fails to go deeply enough. We must also find out the *why* of our feelings. Why do I have such strong feelings of despair (or fear, or anger) when this or that happens? What are the inordinate desires that are being frustrated? What are the idols and false beliefs behind them?

Telling someone (or yourself) that "God loves you, so rejoice!" is insufficient, because you still hold a belief that says, "Even if God loves you but you don't have this particular thing that you treasure, you are still a failure."

You must replace this belief by repenting for the sin beneath it all—your particular idolatry.

The "gospel" approach

Basic analysis: Your problem is that you are looking to something besides Christ for your happiness. You have been worshiping an idol and rejecting the true God. Repent and rejoice!

This approach confronts a person with the real sin underlying the particular sins and behind the bad feelings. Our problem is that we have given ourselves over to idols. Every idol-system is a way of our-works-salvation, and thus it keeps us "under the law."

Paul tells us that the bondage of sin is broken when we come out from under the law—when we begin to believe the gospel of Christ's-work-salvation. Only when we realize in a new way that we are righteous in Christ does the idol's power over us break. "Sin shall not be your master, because you are not under law, but under grace" (Rom. 6:14).

You will only be "under grace" and free from the controlling effects of idols to the degree that you have both (1) repented of your idols and (2) rested and rejoiced in the saving work and love of Christ instead.

To replace idols, you must learn to rejoice in the particular thing Jesus provides that replaces that particular idol of your heart. Whenever you see your heart in the grip of some kind of disobedience or misery, some temptation, anxiety, anger, etc., always ask, (1) How are these effects being caused by an inordinate hope for someone or something to give me what only Jesus can really give me? and (2) How does Christ give me so much more fully and graciously and suitably the very things I am looking for elsewhere? Next, rejoice and consider what he has done and what he has given you. Thomas Chalmers understood this when he wrote in *The Expulsive Power of a New Affection*,

> It is seldom that any of our [bad habits or flaws] are made to disappear by a mere process of natural extinction. At least, it is very seldom that this is done through the instrumentality of reasoning…[or by] the mere force of mental determination. But what cannot be thus destroyed may be dispossessed—and one taste may be made to give way to another, and to lose its power entirely as the reigning affection

Home Study to prepare for Session 3

of the mind… [T]he heart['s]…desire for having some one object or other, this is unconquerable… [T]he only way to dispossess [the heart] of an old affection is by the expulsive power of a new one… It is…when admitted into the number of God's children, through the faith that is in Jesus Christ, [that] the spirit of adoption is poured upon us—it is then that the heart, brought under the mastery of one great and predominant affection, is delivered from the tyranny of its former desires, and is the only way in which deliverance is possible.[8]

Look at the answers you gave in the "Identifying your idols" section. Pray that you would be able to repent of your idols and rejoice in the saving love of Jesus, that you would look only to Christ for your salvation and identity, and that you would be able to break the power your idols hold over you. The following may help you to pray.

Name the idols

In prayer, name these things to God. Sample prayer language:

"Lord, these are the things I have built my life and heart around… "

Repent of the idols

Recognize how weak and poor they are (in themselves). In prayer, confess that these things are good, but finite and weak, and praise God for being the only source of what you need. Sample prayer language:

"Lord, this is a good thing, yet why have I made it so absolute? What is this compared to you? If I have you, I don't have to have this. This cannot love me and help me as you do. This is not my life—Jesus is my life. This is not my righteousness and worthiness. It cannot give me that—but you can and have!"

Recognize how dangerous they are (to you). Idols enslave, and they will never be satisfied. Realize how they increasingly destroy you. In prayer, confess that these things are lethal, and ask a strong God for his help. Sample prayer language:

"Lord, why am I giving this so much power over me? If I keep doing it, it will strangle me. I don't have to do so—I will not do so any longer. This will not be my master. You are my only King."

[8] Thomas Chalmers, "The Expulsive Power of a New Affection" in *The Protestant Pulpit*, ed. Andrew W. Blackwood (New York: Abingdon Press, 1947), 52–56.

Recognize how grievous they are (to Christ). Realize that when you pine after idols (in your anger, fear, despondency), you are saying, "Lord, you are not enough. This is more beautiful, fulfilling, and sweet to my taste than you. You are negotiable, but this is not." In prayer, admit how deeply you have grieved and devalued Jesus, and ask forgiveness. Sample prayer language:

> "Lord, I see how repulsive idolizing this mere idol really is. In yearning after this, I was trampling on your love for me. I realize now my lack of thankfulness, my lack of grateful joy for what you have done for me."

Rejoice in Christ

The following prayers will not affect you unless—as you pray and praise and meditate—the Spirit inscribes the gospel truths on your heart. It is not only important to spend time repenting and rejoicing in fixed times of solitude and prayer; you must also "catch" your heart when it begins falling into idolatry during the day, and you must draw on your hard work of reflection by learning to quickly repent/rejoice your heart into shape on the spot.

Sample rejoicing prayer for times of temptation:

> "Lord, only in your presence are fullness of joy and pleasures forever more (Ps. 16:11), yet here am I trying to find comfort in something else. This thing I am tempted by is just a pleasure that will wear off so soon, while your pleasure, though it may start small, will grow on and on forever (Prov. 4:18). Please remove my idol of pleasure, which can never give me the pleasure I need."

Meditate on John 6, verses 5–13 and 32–40.

Sample rejoicing prayer for times of anxiety:

> "Lord, I live by your sheer grace. That means though I don't deserve to have things go right, yet I know you are working them all out for good (Rom. 8:28), because you love me in Christ. My security in life is based neither on luck nor hard work, but on your gracious love for me. You have counted every hair on my head

(Matt. 10:30–31) and every tear down my cheeks (Ps. 56:8). You love me far more and better than anyone else loves me, or than I love myself. Please remove my idol of security, which can never give me the security I need."

Meditate on Luke 8:22–25 and Mark 4:35–41.

Sample rejoicing prayer for times of anger:

"Lord, when I forget the gospel I become impatient and judgmental toward others. I forget that you have been infinitely patient with me over the years. You are 'slow to anger and rich in love' (Ps. 145:8). When I am anything other than tenderhearted and compassionate to people around me, I am like the unmerciful servant, who, having been forgiven an infinite debt, is hard toward his fellow debtor (Matt. 18:21–35). Please remove the idol of power—the need to get my own way—which is making me so hard toward these people."

Meditate on Matthew 26:36–46.

Sample rejoicing prayer for times of struggling with rejection and a sense of worthlessness:

"Lord, when I forget the gospel I become dependent on the smiles and evaluation of others. I let them sit in judgment on me, and then I hear all their criticism as a condemnation of my very being. But you have said there is no condemnation for me now (Rom. 8:1). You delight and sing over me (Zeph. 3:14–17). Let me be satisfied with your love (Ps. 90:14). Please remove my idol of approval, which can never give me the approval I need."

Meditate on John 15:9–17 and 17:13–26.

You may have other idols besides the four mentioned above. For example, you may have a particular problem with guilt over the past, or with boredom, and so on. Follow the same pattern you see above: How does Jesus particularly provide what the idol cannot? Pray to him, thanking him for his provision, and find some passage of the Bible in which he very visibly and concretely demonstrates this gift or quality. Meditate on it.

Additional Reading

See **gospelinlife.com** for recommended resources to help you further explore this topic.

Session 3 Idolatry The Sin Beneath The Sin

Summary Of The Previous Session

[*Pray as you begin, asking God to be at work in the group.*]

[*Read the paragraphs below aloud to summarize the main points of the previous session.*]

Last session we looked at the parable of the two lost sons in Luke 15 and saw that there are two ways to be your own savior and lord, just as there were two ways the sons tried get the father's things. One son tried to do it by living a bad life, the other by living a good life. We concluded that there are three ways to relate to God—irreligion, religion, and the gospel. The irreligious don't repent at all. The religious only repent of sins. But Christians repent of both their sins and of their righteousness.

We also saw that religion is the default mode of the human heart and that behavioral compliance to rules without heart-change will be superficial and fleeting. It is only an ever deepening faith in the gospel that restructures our motivations, our self-understanding and identity, and our view of the world. Only the gospel changes our hearts.

This session we continue the theme of gospel and the heart by looking at how and why our hearts construct idols.

[*Take 3 to 5 minutes to briefly discuss the Home Study on pages 36–50. Mention anything you found helpful, new, exciting, or confusing.*]

Bible Study

[*Read aloud Romans 1:18–25 and then work through the questions below.*]

1. What is the reason that our minds and hearts become "futile" and "darkened"? (Look especially at verse 21a.)

2. According to these verses, what are some of the results of idolatry in our lives? Has this been true in your own experience? Share examples.

3. What do these verses tell us about the wrath of God?

4. John Calvin describes us as "a perpetual factory of idols."[1] What are some examples of personal idols?

[*Watch the DVD for Session 3.*]

DVD Notes

[*Use this space if you would like to make notes.*]

[1] John Calvin, *Institutes of the Christian Religion*, Battles Edition, Book 1, Chapter XI, Section 8 (Philadelphia: Westminster Press, 1960), 108.

Discussion Questions

1. Was there anything from the DVD that was new to you, or had an effect on you? Did you hear anything that raised more questions in your mind?

2. "If you really want to change…Jesus Christ must become your over-mastering positive passion." When and how have you found this to be true in your experience or in the lives of people you know?

3. Archbishop William Temple said, "Your religion is what you do with your solitude."[2] When you are alone what do you tend to think about most? Where do your thoughts go naturally, instinctively, habitually? How does this help identify your idols?

4. "Under every behavioral sin is the sin of idolatry, and under every act of idolatry is a disbelief in the gospel." Do you agree? Why or why not? What are the implications for how we really change our hearts and lives?

[2] This quote is attributed to Sir William Temple, English diplomat, statesman, essayist and author (1628–1699).

5. In his book *Gods That Fail*, Vinoth Ramachandra quotes Psalm 115 on idols: "Those who make them will be like them, and so will all who trust in them." He writes, "Note the shattering conclusion: we become like what we worship."[3] Do we? In what way and why?

6. What are some of the concrete ways we can make Christ King and Lord of our entire lives?

Prayer

See the *Home Study* on pages 47–49 to help you pray that you would be able to repent of your idols and rejoice in the saving love of Jesus.

Introduction Of The Home Study

To introduce you to Session 4, the *Home Study* consists of a series of readings and exercises about affirming others, sharing, and serving in your Christian community.

[3] Vinoth Ramachandra, *Gods That Fail* (Downers Grove, Ill.: IVP, 1996), 115.

"Princeton's Robert Wuthnow has found that small groups mainly 'provide occasions for individuals to focus on themselves in the presence of others. The social contract binding members together asserts only the weakest of obligations. Come if you have time. Talk if you feel like it. Respect everyone's opinion. Never criticize. Leave quietly if you become dissatisfied.' In *Overcoming Loneliness in Everyday Life*, two Boston psychiatrists... suggest that...groups 'fail to replicate the sense of belonging we have lost. Attending weekly meetings, dropping in and out as one pleases, shopping around for a more satisfactory or appealing group—all of these factors work against the growth of true community.'"[1]

Christians expect to find community by attending church services and coming to a small group. As the quote above points out, however, it is possible to hold a weekly small group meeting without adding the elements that create real community. Because of our idols and the habits of our heart church events simply become places that individuals "focus on themselves in the presence of others." It takes deep reflection and costly commitment to live in community. Use this Home Study to help you think about what a Christian community really is.

Home Study to prepare for Session 4

The theology of community

What is a Christian community? This question has three primary answers.

1. The people of God—those who are created by faith through his gospel

A Christian community consists of those who have repented and believed and have a common experience of the gospel, which is a message of grace.

The controlling biblical metaphor for this is the "assembly" at Mount Sinai. There God said, "You yourselves have seen what I did to Egypt, and how I carried you on eagles' wings and brought you to myself. Now if you obey me fully and keep my covenant, then out of all nations you will be my treasured possession" (Ex. 19:4–5). "I will free you from being slaves to them, and I will redeem you… I will take you as my own people, and I will be your God" (Ex. 6:6–7). Notice the order in Exodus 19:4–5. First God saves them from slavery and secondly, as a result, they now obey his law and live according to his will. They do not first obey the law and, as a result of their merit, God saves them. They were saved by grace, committed themselves to God, and so became a distinct "people." What made the Israelites "a people"—a corporate body, a community—was a shared past of God's grace.

This remains true for Christians today. In the New Testament, 1 Peter 2:9–10 deliberately takes phrases from Exodus 19:4–6 and applies them to the church. We too are "a people belonging to God" (1 Peter 2:9), because we have heard and believed the gospel and have been brought into a new relationship with other Christians, now our "brothers" (1 Peter 1:22).

2. The body of Christ—those who are members of one another in his life

A Christian community, secondly, consists of people who deliberately share life together.

The controlling biblical metaphor for this aspect is that Christians are God's "family" and "household" (Gal. 6:10; Eph. 2:19; 1 Peter 4:17; Rom. 12:10). A family shares all of life together, eating, living, and working together. The other controlling metaphor is "the body," another powerful way of saying that

[1] Quoted in Randy Frazee, *The Connecting Church: Beyond Small Groups to Authentic Community* (Grand Rapids, Mich.: Zondervan, 2001), 46–47.

Christians are not an aggregation of individuals but a coherent organism, with each member playing his or her part and deeply, integrally connected to the rest.

3. The fellowship of the Spirit—those who are a model of his future

Thirdly, a Christian Spirit-filled community is an alternative society that models distinctive ways to do everything in life.

One of the controlling biblical metaphors for this is the church as a "city on a hill" (Matt. 5:14), whose visible behavior shines out and shows the world the glory of God.

In the future, God is going to unite and heal all things under the lordship of Christ (Eph. 1:9–10; Isa. 11:1–9.) In Ephesians 1:13–14, Paul writes that the Spirit is a "deposit guaranteeing" that future restoration. Currently, the church is to model what that future society under Christ will look like. We are to model the transformation that the gospel makes to every area of life.

Becoming the sort of community described above requires creative community-building strategies. Read the following which will help you think through some of them.

A biblical survey of community-building practices

Paul says that in Christ's body, "each member belongs to all the others" (Rom. 12:5). This goes deeper than the modern concept of being a "member" of a club, because the Greek word he uses, *melos*, was the common word for a part of the human body. Paul is saying, "You are the limbs and organs of one another. You are the eyes, arms, and heart of one another." We are profoundly interdependent.

The implications of this principle are spelled out practically in dozens of "one another" passages in the New Testament epistles. The following are nine "community-building practices"—specific behaviors that build Christian community.

Home Study to prepare for Session 4

The first three practices are all about affirming one another—about how to be friends.

Practice 1—affirming one another's strengths, abilities, and gifts

- Romans 12:10 – "Honor one another"
- James 5:9 – "Don't grumble against each other"
- Romans 12:3–8 – Confirm the gifts of one another

This first community-building practice is expressed especially in Romans 12:10, "Honor one another above yourselves." That is, be much more concerned to praise, affirm, honor, and celebrate others than you are to receive the same.

Christians should be people who are quick to praise and celebrate what others have done, who love to praise, appreciate, and make supportive statements.

More specifically, it is a deliberate practice of identifying the following in others:

- Where they are growing and making progress. (Do you see them growing in their ability to handle problems, difficulties, and criticism? Do you see them growing in peace, joy, or self-control? Affirm and speak to them about it.)

- What talents and gifts they have that benefit others. (Do you see them ministering in ways that benefit others spiritually? If you see a pattern to how they do it, is that a gift or talent they should be cultivating? Affirm and speak to them about it.)

- Which sacrifices they are making to do the right thing, even though others may not be aware of it. (Are they perhaps making great sacrifices just to honor God? Notice the ongoing sacrifices and affirm their obedience.)

Fruit, gifts, and sacrifices are to be confirmed and affirmed in community. All of this gives "honor" to others (Rom. 12:10).

Notes on specific texts:

- Romans 12:1–8, taken as a whole, indicates that we should appreciate one another's very distinctive gifts and abilities, not despising those who are different.

- The opposite of an affirming, honoring spirit is what James 5:9 alludes to. There the word "grumble" means literally to sigh or groan. You can show exasperation and disdain in a way that makes others feel not simply critiqued, but small and marginalized.

Practice 2—affirming one another's equal importance in Christ

- Romans 15:7 – "Accept one another, then, just as Christ accepted you"
- 1 Corinthians 12:25 – "Have equal concern for each other"
- 1 Peter 5:5 – "Clothe yourselves with humility toward one another"
- James 2:1 – "Don't show favoritism"

This is a general mind-set that refuses to be impressed with the world's status-ladders or pecking orders. In the world, some classes, races, vocations, and cultures have more power than others, but the Bible calls us in numerous places to refuse to let those distinctions enter the church. Specifically, it is the practice of deliberately building relationships with other Christians across traditional cultural barriers.

Saul's conversion story demonstrates this aspect of the character of Christian community. In Acts, Saul's initial attitude toward Christians is "murderous" (Acts 9:1). He happily supports the stoning of Stephen (Acts 8:1) and wants to see more of the same, so he travels to Damascus to arrest anyone he finds there who is a believer in Jesus. Ananias, a Christian in Damascus, knows about Saul's expedition and realizes he is likely to be arrested and perhaps killed by Saul (Acts 9:14).

Suddenly Ananias gets a word from the Lord that the murderer/persecutor has been converted to faith in Christ and that Ananias is to go to Saul. Though understandably fearful, Ananias immediately obeys. "Placing his hands on Saul, he said, 'Brother Saul, the Lord...has sent me'" (Acts 9:17).

Considering how small the church still was, it is almost certain that Saul had arrested and maybe killed people Ananias had known and loved. Yet the gospel destroys the old ties and identities, and now that Saul believes in Christ, he is immediately Ananias' brother! Ananias is essentially saying, "Ultimately it doesn't matter who you were and what you've done. Because of Christ we are brothers."

Racism, classism, and cultural imperialism must be rooted out of our hearts with the gospel. Put another way: if you would rather have your Christian friend/relative marry a person of the same race, class, or status regardless of their religious convictions, instead of marrying a solid Christian of a different race, class, or status, your prejudices have not been gospel-changed.

Notes on specific texts:

- 1 Corinthians 12 recognizes that many people have "greater" gifts (e.g., speaking ability, leadership ability), which tend to attract greater honor in the world—but within the church, verse 25 says, every member must be treated with (literally) "equal anxiety." We are to be equally accepting, welcoming, and concerned for everyone.
- James 2:1–14 is a classic text that forbids favoring the rich over the poor.

Practice 3—affirming one another through visible affection

- Romans 16:16 – "Greet one another with a holy kiss"
- James 1:19 – "Be quick to listen, slow to speak"
- Ephesians 4:32 – "Be kind and compassionate to one another"
- 1 Thessalonians 3:12 – "Your love increase and overflow for each other"

There are a number of directions in the New Testament to "Greet one another with a holy kiss" (Rom. 16:16; 1 Cor. 16:20; 2 Cor. 13:12) or "with a kiss of love" (1 Peter 5:14). It is customary to skip over these verses with the thought that this was an ancient cultural greeting that we don't use any more. Even if we grant the need for some cultural translation to our own time, that does not remove our responsibility to obey the biblical command to communicate love and affection in a visible way. It is appropriate for different people groups to choose different ways to communicate love and affection, but they must do it.

We must not be cold, clipped, abrupt, indifferent, and harsh with one another. More than that, we must be willing to actually talk about our love for each other.

Notes on specific texts:

- James 1:19 says one of the easiest ways to practice and show warmth is to listen very attentively to others, rather than being quick to talk.

Use the following questions to help you think through these first three practices.

1. **Which of these three categories of community-building are you and your group currently the best at? Why? Which of these three categories are you and your group currently the worst at? Why? What can you do to get better?**

2. **John Stott writes,**

God means his church to be a community of mutual support. "Comfort one another", Paul writes (1 Thess. 4:18); "encourage one another," and "build each other up" (1 Thess. 5:11)... The word "one another" or "each other" (*alleloi*) emphasizes the reciprocity of Christian care. We are not to leave it to an elite of professional comforters or counselors. These have an important role to fulfill, of course, but supporting, caring, encouraging and comforting are ministries which belong to all members of the Body of Christ.[2]

Do you agree with his assessment? Write down some specific ways and some specific people you and your group can support, care, encourage, and comfort.

3. In *Life Together* Dietrich Bonhoeffer writes,

The first service that one owes to others in the fellowship consists in listening to them. Just as love to God begins with listening to His Word, so the beginning of love for [others] is learning to listen to them… Listening can be greater service than speaking… There is a kind of listening…an impatient, inattentive listening, that…is only waiting for a chance to speak and thus get rid of the other person.[3]

How can you and your group get better at listening? Are there times when or people with whom you find this difficult? Why and what can you do to change?

[2] John Stott, *The Message of 1 and 2 Thessalonians* (Downers Grove, Ill.: IVP, 1991), 115. [3] Dietrich Bonhoeffer, *Life Together* (New York: Harper, 1954), 97–98.

The next three community-building practices are all about sharing with one another—about how to be family.

Practice 4—sharing one another's space, goods, and time

- Romans 12:10 – "Be devoted to one another in brotherly love"
- 1 Peter 4:9 – "Offer hospitality to one another"
- Galatians 6:10 – "As we have opportunity, let us do good"

This is a willingness to share one's physical, material world with others, the way family members do.

Specifically, this practice includes:

- Sharing space with one another. Christians are to invite one another into their living space. They are to share life together. This means eating, studying, playing, praying, and so on—together.
- Sharing one another's goods. In the most practical way, we help one another. It may mean doing practical errands, giving financial gifts, or providing for needs in other concrete ways.
- Sharing common time together. This means both being available to one another as well as a commitment to meeting together with regularity.

Notes on specific texts:

- Any place that the text reads we are to "do good" to one another (e.g., Gal. 6:10), it is speaking of very concrete material help. It means providing money, shelter, or other practical help.

Practice 5—sharing one another's needs and problems

- Galatians 6:2 – "Carry each other's burdens"
- 1 Thessalonians 5:11 – "Encourage one another"
- Hebrews 3:13 – "Encourage one another daily"

Sharing resources and possessions is one way to become vulnerable to others in a community. Another way is to share with others our grief and weakness

Home Study to prepare for Session 4

and allow them to give us their love and support. We are to be willing to find people who are hurting and offer whatever support they need.

Notes on specific texts:

- 1 Thessalonians 5:11 and many other passages call us to "encourage" one another. The Greek means to come very close and cheer and support the person in a journey.

- Galatians 6:2 tells us to carry one another's burdens. Picture how you help a person who is trying to carry a load that is too heavy. To help with a burden, you must first come very close to the burdened person, standing virtually in their shoes. Next, you must put your own strength under the burden so its weight is distributed on both of you, thus lightening the load for the original bearer. To "carry the burden" means to come under it and let some of its weight, responsibility, and pain come onto you.

There is a hidden reciprocity in Galatians 6:2 that should not be overlooked. Notice it does not say "carry other's burdens" but "carry each other's burdens." It means something like this: "Live in a community where you don't let others carry their loads alone, and where you also don't try to carry your own load alone. Help others and let others help you." It is a form of hypocrisy to be willing to help others with their weaknesses but to hide your own or refuse help. It takes a gospel-changed heart to give help unselfishly to others, and it takes a gospel-changed heart to receive help unashamedly from others.

Galatians 6:2 then expands this thought. "Carry each other's burdens, and in this way you will fulfill the law of Christ." Obviously, Christ is the ultimate example of burden-bearing love. He bore the infinite burden of our guilt and sin on the cross, and it crushed him. He did not simply share that burden with us, he completely freed us from it by bearing its entire weight. Anyone who knows this infinite, burden-bearing love has a breathtaking model who inspires and empowers us into the same kind of love.

Practice 6—sharing one another's beliefs, thinking, and spirituality

- Colossians 3:16 – "Teach and admonish one another"
- Ephesians 5:19 – "Speak to one another with psalms, hymns and spiritual songs"
- Romans 12:16 – "Live in harmony with one another"
- 1 Corinthians 1:10 – "Agree with one another"

This is all about developing unity of mind and heart in the gospel. Christians are called to study and teach the Bible to one another, to pray and sing God's praises with one another. All of this has the effect of creating unity of belief and heart in the gospel. Ephesians 4:14–16 says we are not "blown here and there by every wind of teaching... Instead, speaking the truth in love...the whole body [is] joined and held together."

We are not simply to study the Bible as individuals; we are to read and argue and study the Bible together to come to deeper unity of faith and to consensus about how to be the people of God in our particular time and place. We are to read the Bible together until it shapes us as a distinct community.

Notes on specific texts:

- When Paul urges us to "teach and admonish one another with all wisdom" (Col. 3:16), the verbs are to "instruct" and to "challenge" or "confront." This would certainly include holding people to obey the Bible but the Greek word for "instruct one another" means more than that. It means working together to understand the implications of the Word of God for our life together. We are being directed to read, discuss, mutually instruct, challenge, and make reasoned arguments about the Bible together until it shapes the way we live together.

Use the following questions to help you think through the second three practices.

1. Which of these three categories of community-building are you and your group currently the best at? Why? Which of these three categories are you and your group currently the worst at? Why? What can you do to get better?

2. In his book *Neither Poverty Nor Riches* Craig Blomberg writes,

> The only way God's people can consistently obey all of his commands is as the entire Christian community worldwide, and any local expression of it increasingly captures the vision of sharing its resources with the needy in its midst. When believers realize that others will care for them if they unexpectedly find themselves impoverished, they can then be freed to give more generously in times of plenty.[4]

Do you agree with his assessment? Do you and your group have a "vision of sharing your resources with the needy in your midst"? How can you develop that more?

3. In *Life Together* Dietrich Bonhoeffer writes,

> The second service that one should perform for another in a Christian community is that of active helpfulness. This means, initially, simple assistance in trifling, external matters... We must be ready to allow ourselves to be interrupted by God. God will be constantly canceling our plans by sending us people with claims and petitions. We may pass them by, preoccupied with our more important tasks, as the priest passed the man who had fallen among thieves, perhaps—reading the Bible.[5]

How do you and your group feel when your plans are canceled by "people with claims and petitions"? Write down some specific ways you could share space, goods, time, needs, problems.

[4] Craig Blomberg, *Neither Poverty Nor Riches: A Biblical Theology of Possessions* (Leicester, England: Apollos, 1999), 145. [5] Dietrich Bonhoeffer, *Life Together* (New York: Harper, 1954), 99.

The last three community-building practices are all about serving one another—about how to be servants.

Practice 7—serving one another through accountability

- James 5:16 – "Confess your sins to each other and pray for each other"
- Romans 15:14 – "Instruct one another"
- Ephesians 4:25 – "Speak truthfully"

Earlier we mentioned that we must be willing to let others in the community know about our problems or needs. Even more specifically, we must allow ourselves to be accountable to others to live as we should, even in the more personal aspects. In particular, we must be willing to admit where we have besetting sins and look to the Christian community to help us overcome them. We must voluntarily develop a circle of Christian friends to whom we are regularly accountable for areas of behavior that are especially difficult, or in which self-deception is easy. For example, life balance (work, health, and rest), sexuality, use of money, and so on.

We must work out in community what a gospel-shaped life should be, and then allow ourselves to be held accountable to live in this way. We are to let our Christian friends into our lives deeply enough to see our weaknesses and hold us responsible to grow into Christ's likeness.

Note on specific texts:

- James 5:16 is the only place where we are told to confess our sins to others. Some have concluded, because of the context, that this is only for people who are seeking healing from physical illness. Hebrews 3:13, however, tells us to "encourage one another daily," lest we be "hardened by sin's deceitfulness" (i.e., hiddenness). Such a practice certainly entails having a fairly intimate knowledge of one another's flaws.
- Romans 15:14 uses a word, *noutheo*, which means "to admonish," to lovingly confront someone.

Home Study to prepare for Session 4

Practice 8—serving one another through forgiveness and reconciliation

- Ephesians 4:2 – "Be completely humble and gentle; be patient, bearing with one another in love"
- Colossians 3:13 – "Forgive whatever grievances you may have against one another"
- Galatians 5:26 – Don't provoke or envy one another
- James 4:11 – "Do not slander one another"
- Matthew 5:23–24; 18:15 – Reestablish broken relationships with one another

Christians in community are never to give up on one another. We must never tire of forgiving (and/or repenting) and seeking to repair our relationships. Matthew 5:23–24 tells us we should go to someone if we know the person has something against us. Matthew 18:15 says we should approach others if we know that we have something against them. In short, it is always your move to repair relationships in the community. God always holds you responsible to reach out to repair a broken relationship. A Christian is responsible to begin the process of reconciliation, regardless of how the distance or the alienation began.

Notes on the texts:

- Ephesians 4:2 is a general directive, telling us to "bear with" one another. This means being patient and forbearing over small irritations.
- Galatians 5:26 uses two words that have the opposite meaning. To "provoke" means basically to despise someone, to look down and disdain someone because the person has less (intelligence, appropriate views, proper behavior, looks, status) than you. To "envy" means to feel inferior to, to resent because someone has more (intelligence, education, looks, status, power) than you. Both kinds of attitudes breed conflicts and unreconciled relationships.
- James 4:11 forbids the kind of condemning, judgmental, harsh language and attitudes that break relationships.

Practice 9—serving one another's interests rather than our own

- Hebrews 10:24 – "spur one another on toward love and good deeds"
- Romans 15:1–2 – Don't please yourself but please others
- Galatians 5:13 – "Serve one another"

This is a general mind-set of putting the needs and interests of others in the community ahead of your own. It is the classic servant-heart. This means to look deliberately for needs around you, of all sorts, and find ways to meet them through loving deeds, seeking as little in the way of recognition as possible.

We are not to enter into community-building simply to make ourselves feel needed or connected. It is possible to exploit others in Christian community. One way is by making ourselves so indispensable to others that we become dependent on others' dependence on us. Another way is by taking—emotionally, materially, and spiritually—from the community and not giving anything back. In Christ we should not be so proud that we believe we don't need community, nor so needy that we exploit others in the community.

Notes on the texts:

- Hebrews 10:24 tells us that we should be giving deliberate consideration to how to build up those around us into Christlikeness.
- Romans 15:1–2 says we are to please them for their good, to build them up.
- Paul boldly tells us to be *douloi* of one another (Gal. 5:13)—literally bond-slaves. Extending the metaphor, Paul says that we owe one another love as a kind of debt (Rom. 13:8). Indentured servants, when they fell into debt, became bond-slaves of their creditors until the debt was paid. Because Christ humbled himself and became a servant and met our needs even at the cost of his own life, now we are like indentured servants—but to one another. We owe everyone a debt of love.

Home Study to prepare for Session 4

Finally, we are to love one another. Notice how often this phrase recurs in the epistles: Romans 12:10, 13:8; 1 Thessalonians 4:9; Hebrews 13:1; 1 Peter 1:22, 4:8; 1 John 3:11, 3:23, 4:7, 4:11; 2 John 1:5. We are to love one another deeply from the heart if any of these practices are to build our community.

Use the following questions to help you think through the last three practices.

1. Which of these three categories of community-building are you and your group currently the best at? Why? Which of these three categories are you and your group currently the worst at? Why? What can you do to get better?

2. In his book *Christ Plays in Ten Thousand Places* Eugene Peterson writes,

> We are a community. We are not ourselves by ourselves. We are born into communities, we live in communities, we die in communities. Human beings are not solitary, self-sufficient creatures.[6]

Do you agree? Do you have a tendency to behave like you are self-sufficient or think of yourself as self-sufficient? When and why? How can you and your group get better at serving one another's interests?

3. In *Life Together* Dietrich Bonhoeffer writes,

> "Confess your faults one to another" (James 5:16.)... A man who confesses his sins in the presence of a brother knows that he is no longer alone with himself; he experiences the presence of God in the reality of the other person.[7]

Do you agree? What keeps you from confessing your faults to others? How can you get better at doing this?

[6] Eugene Peterson, *Christ Plays in Ten Thousand Places* (Grand Rapids, Mich.: Eerdmans, 2005), 239. [7] Dietrich Bonhoeffer, *Life Together* (New York: Harper, 1954), 110–116.

4. In light of your answers to all the questions above, write down two or three practical things you could do this week to improve your community-building practices.

> Pray about each of these nine community-building practices, asking God to give you the desire to affirm others, share, and serve in your community.

Additional Reading

See **gospelinlife.com** for recommended resources to help you further explore this topic.

Session 4 Community The Context For Change

Summary Of The Previous Session

[*Pray as you begin, asking God to be at work in the group.*]

[*Read the paragraphs below aloud to summarize the main points of the previous session.*]

Last session we saw that nothing is to be more fundamental than God to our happiness, meaning in life, and identity. We saw, however, that we easily create idols.

An idol is anything besides Jesus Christ that we feel we must have to be happy, anything that is more important to our heart than God, anything that is enslaving our heart through inordinate desires. Martin Luther said that under every behavioral sin is the sin of idolatry, and under every act of idolatry is a disbelief in the gospel.

As we look now at the idea of a Christian community, keep in mind that idolatry is also one of the key problems we face when it comes to creating community.

[*Take 3 to 5 minutes to briefly discuss the* Home Study *on pages 56–72. Mention anything you found helpful, new, exciting, or confusing.*]

Bible Study

[*Read aloud Philippians 2:1–11 and then work through the questions below.*]

1. Looking at verses 2–4, what can we infer is the problem that Paul is addressing in the Philippian church?

2. What are the four grounds for unity and humility that Paul lists in verse 1? How do these grounds lead to unity and humility?

3. Verse 5 says, "Your attitude should be the same as that of Christ Jesus." What do we learn about Jesus' attitude from verses 6–11?

4. In his book *Love in Hard Places* Don Carson writes,

> The church is...made up of natural enemies. What binds us together is not common education, common race, common income levels, common politics, common nationality, common accents, common jobs, or anything else of that sort. Christians come together...because they have all been saved by Jesus Christ and owe him a common allegiance... They are a band of natural enemies who love one another for Jesus' sake.[1]

Do you agree with his assessment? Why or why not? Share examples.

[*Read aloud 1 Peter 2:9–12 and then* **watch the DVD for Session 4.**]

DVD Notes

[*Use this space if you would like to make notes.*]

---

[1] D. A. Carson, *Love In Hard Places* (Wheaton, Ill.: Crossway, 2002), 61.

Discussion Questions

1. Was there anything from the DVD that was new to you, or had an effect on you? Did you hear anything that raised more questions in your mind?

2. We heard in the DVD that,

   > We are "a holy nation"—different, distinct from the world and the people around us. And yet at the same time, we're supposed to be "a royal priesthood"— deeply involved in the lives of the world and the people around us.

   Do you feel that you are part of the sort of community described in the DVD? If not, why not? What can you do to make this happen?

3. "We will not know God, change deeply, nor win the world apart from community." To what extent have you experienced this?

4. What practices make a good, strong, healthy Christian community? Brainstorm practical ways by which your own group can deepen its life together as a community.

5. How can we love people we do not naturally like?

6. Look at the following list derived from Romans 12.

Love honestly, speaking out against what is wrong. (v. 9)
Love even unattractive people, because they are your brothers and sisters. (v. 10)
Love by making others feel honored and valuable. (v. 10)
Love by being generous in practical ways with your home, money, and time. (v. 13)
Love without bitterness. Don't "pay others back," or hold resentment against others. (v. 14)
Love with empathy. Be willing to be emotionally involved with others. (v. 15)
Love with humility. Be willing to associate with people who differ from you. (v. 16)

In which areas do you, as a group, tend to be the weakest, and why? What practical steps could you take to improve?

Prayer

Thank God for your Christian community and pray for Christ's love to ignite your heart to love, share with, and serve others continually. Pray that you would be the sort of community you discussed through this study.

Session 4 Community The Context For Change

Introduction Of The Home Study

As a community, we not only speak the gospel, we live it through hospitality and deeds of love and kindness. This session's *Home Study* is to plan an event as a group to which you can invite your non-Christian friends and work colleagues. This is an opportunity for your friends to spend time with your Christian community, and for you as a community to practice hospitality.

In the Old Testament, hospitality is part of normal and common practice. For example, in Genesis 18 Abraham is quick and ready to offer hospitality to the strangers who arrive near his home. When Jesus sends out the twelve disciples, he expects that they will be shown hospitality (Mark 6:8–11). We are also called to "Practice hospitality" (Rom. 12:13) and to "Offer hospitality to one another" (1 Peter 4:9). This verse also tells us to do hospitality "without grumbling." Genesis 18:5 tells us the goal of the one giving hospitality is to refresh and encourage others. Hospitality done well is generous, uncomplaining, loving, and refreshing. It does not make guests feel like "guests" but like members of a family. Hospitality provides a feeling of security, warmth, safety, and love.

As you plan your event, think about atmosphere, the process of welcoming guests, food—everything that will make your guests feel relaxed and comfortable. This event will involve time, planning, and prayer.

Ideas for events:

- Watch a sport—either live or on TV
- Play a sport
- Go to an event (e.g., theater, museum exhibit, art gallery exhibit, and so on)
- Plan a trip to the beach or to an historical monument
- Put together a movie night
- Organize a meal at someone's home, or a barbecue, or a dinner at a new restaurant
- Get together to watch a special event on TV (e.g., an election, an awards show)
- If a member of the group has a skill or talent, organize an activity around that (e.g., some kind of art or dance class)

- If a group member is trained in a particular area, plan an event around that expertise (e.g., a talk on parenting or stress or fashion or whatever topic would interest your friends)
- If your church is planning events that would suit your friends, invite them to those (e.g., a talk on marriage enrichment or financial planning)
- Organize an event around a specific current news issue that everyone is discussing and give a Christian viewpoint on the topic (e.g., a debate on a current bestseller)

If for whatever reason you cannot plan an event, then pick a Sunday service for your group to attend together and invite your friends and work colleagues to it. Have a meal or coffee together after the service.

As a group, decide on the type of event you would like to host and when in the following weeks you are able to host it. Make a list of action steps for the event and divide these responsibilities among the group members.

Event:		
Date:		
To Do	Date to be completed	Name of person responsible

Pray for your event, for all the preparations necessary, for your friends to come, and for God to use the event to further his kingdom and bring more people into his household.

"For Christians, a delight in the guest/host relationship reflects the expectation that God will play a significant role in the ordinary exchange between guests and hosts. This lends to hospitality a sacramental quality… The allusion to those who entertained angels as their guests without knowing it [Hebrews 13:2] reflects the writer's sensitivity to the numinous qualities of hospitality that often enrich its purely social aspects."[1]

At your last meeting your group will have decided to host an event to which you can invite your non-Christian friends and work colleagues. Remember, it is an opportunity for your friends to spend time with your Christian community and for you as a community to practice hospitality. Look at the table on page 79 and carry out the task assigned to you. Spend some time praying for the event, for all the preparations necessary, and for God to graciously use it to bring people into the Christian community. Use this Home Study *to help you prepare for the event.*

Home Study to prepare for Session 5

Oikos evangelism

As the event approaches, you will need to be thinking of people to invite. When extending an invitation, it is important to be honest and clear about exactly what will happen and who will be at the event. Do not hide the fact that it is being organized by your Christian community.

As you invite people, they may begin to question you about your beliefs. Even if they do not attend the event, the invitation itself may give you an opportunity to share something of the gospel with them. After the event your friends may likely have additional questions about the Christian faith and what it means to be a part of a Christian community.

It may be helpful to remember that in the book of Acts, the main method of evangelism is "household evangelism." Look up Acts 10:24; 16:15, 31; and 18:8. *Oikos*, the Greek word for "household," means far more than the nuclear family. A Greco-Roman household included not only several generations of the same family, but also servants, their families, friends, and business associates.

An *oikos* is a web of relationships held in common

- kinship affinity (relatives)
- geographical affinity (neighbors)
- professional affinity (coworkers)
- associational affinities (special interest colleagues)
- just plain friends.

In *oikos* evangelism

- Your life is under observation by those who don't believe.
- Your life is the attractor and evidence for the truth of the faith. People should get a very good view of how Christianity works in a life.
- The other person is "in the driver's seat." They get to raise questions and determine the speed of the process.
- The humbling nature of the gospel leads us to approach people without superiority and with deep respect.

[1] William Lane, *Word Biblical Commentary: Hebrews 9–13* (Dallas, Tex.: Word Books, 1991), 512–513.

[*As the event approaches, what things can you do to prepare for* oikos *evangelism?*]

[*List five people in your* oikos *(see above for the types of relationships)*]

1.	
2.	
3.	
4.	
5.	

[*Begin to pray for them regularly, and plan to invite them to your event.*]

Additional Reading

See **gospelinlife.com** for recommended resources to help you further explore this topic.

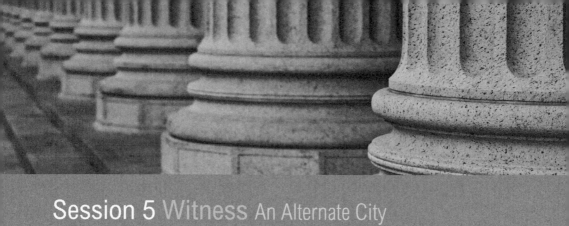

Session 5 Witness An Alternate City

Summary Of The Previous Session

[*Pray as you begin, asking God to be at work in the group.*]

[*Read the paragraphs below aloud to summarize the main points of the previous session.*]

Last session we saw that the church is "a royal priesthood, a holy nation, a people belonging to God" (1 Peter 2:9). It is a new humanity, a new community of people under the lordship of Christ.

We need to create a great community because that is, according to Jesus in John 17 verses 20–23, a crucial way to show the world that we are truly followers of Christ. In fact, we saw that we will not know God, change deeply, or win the world apart from community.

This session continues the theme of gospel and community, and looks at how we witness as a community.

[*Take 3 to 5 minutes to pray and discuss arrangements for the event you are planning (see pages 78–82).*]

Bible Study

> *Read aloud Acts 2:42–47 which describes the early church, and then work through the questions below.*

1. What do we discover about how the early church learned together? What do we discover about fellowship and service? What can we learn from this?

2. The early church were so involved with each other that they had fellowship "every day." Do you have fellowship with another Christian every day? Is this possible? Why or why not?

3. What do we discover about how the early church worshiped and how they witnessed to others? What can we learn from this?

4. British theologian Lesslie Newbigin observes:

The gospel does not become public truth for a society by being propagated as a theory or as a worldview and certainly not as a religion. It can become public truth only insofar as it is embodied in a society (the church) which is both "abiding in" Christ and engaged in the life of the world.[1]

Do you agree with his assessment? Why or why not? Share examples.

[*Watch the DVD for Session 5.*]

DVD Notes

[*Use this space if you would like to make notes.*]

---

[1] Lesslie Newbigin, *Proper Confidence: Faith, Doubt and Certainty in Christian Discipleship* (Grand Rapids, Mich.: Eerdmans, 1995), 39.

Session 5 Witness An Alternate City

Discussion Questions

1. Was there anything from the DVD that was new to you, or had an effect on you? Did you hear anything that raised more questions in your mind?

2. "An alternate city is gospel-speaking." What intimidates us about telling other people about Jesus? Are some people more intimidating than others? Why? What motivates us to tell people about Jesus?

3. "There is a credibility that comes if you are consistent in your behavior, there is a credibility that comes if people see the gospel transforming you." Do people notice your lifestyle and that of your community? Do they appreciate it, even if they don't understand it? Share examples.

4. Frank Retief, a pastor and church planter in South Africa, writes, "people without Christ go to hell—if you really believe that you've got to take risks, take a chance and be prepared to fail."[2] What do you think of his statement?

 [2] Bishop Frank Retief quoted in *Multiplying Churches* edited by Stephen Timmis (Ross-shire, Scotland: Christian Focus Publications, 2000), 97.

5. A leading missiologist, C. Peter Wagner, writes, "Planting new churches is the most effective evangelistic methodology known under heaven."[3] Think of some reasons why starting new churches is a good way to reach people.

6. "When Christ returns to earth, the present age will end completely and the age to come will come fully. Meanwhile, we actually live between the two ages—in what's been called the overlap of the ages." What mistaken thoughts, distorted emotions, or wrong practices result when we don't focus enough on the age to come? What about when we don't focus enough on the present age?

Prayer

Thank God that in the future he is going to unite and heal all things under the lordship of Christ. Pray that your community would be "a city on a hill" (Matt. 5:14). Pray that you, as the community of God's people, would evidence the beauty and visible reality of God. Ask for opportunities to build relationships with and witness to people who don't believe in Christ, and for courage to live the gospel before others.

Introduction Of The Home Study

To introduce you to Session 6, the *Home Study* focuses on the concept of work and how the gospel should have an impact on the way we work and think about our work.

---

[3] C. Peter Wagner, *Strategies for Church Growth* (Ventura, Calif.: Regal, 1987), 168–169.

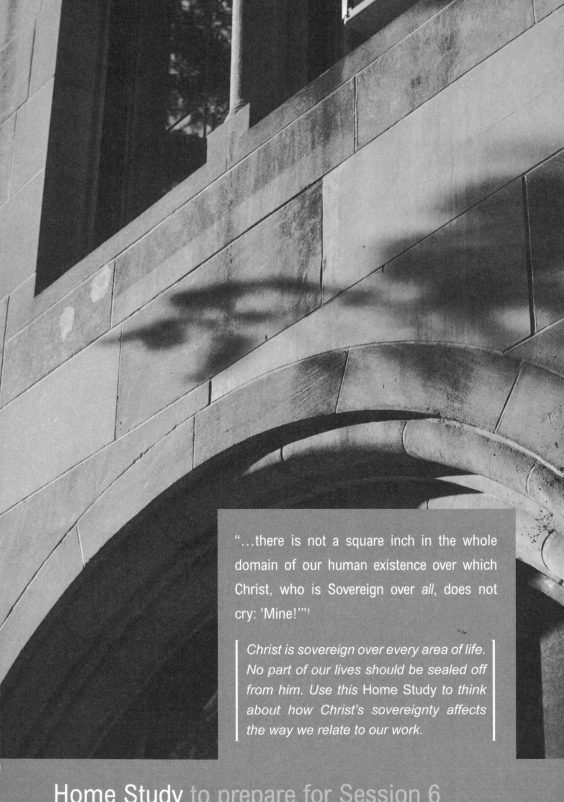

"…there is not a square inch in the whole domain of our human existence over which Christ, who is Sovereign over *all*, does not cry: 'Mine!'"[1]

Christ is sovereign over every area of life. No part of our lives should be sealed off from him. Use this Home Study *to think about how Christ's sovereignty affects the way we relate to our work.*

Home Study to prepare for Session 6

Creation, fall, and our work

Human beings were given work to do (Gen. 2:15) before the fall—before sin and before anything was wrong with the world. Work, therefore, is something we were designed to do.

[*Read Genesis 1–3 and answer the questions below.*]

1. In what ways does God indicate that he revels in his creation? How does that make you feel about creation and about yourself?

2. When the narrative gets to the sixth day, the account shifts into a majestic, first-person plural, "Let us make..." and Adam and Eve are immediately put to work. List the jobs that God mentions.

3. From the very beginning, according to God's own activity, there is a rhythm—a time to speak/work and a time be silent/rest. Why and how should this apply to your life?

4. After the fall, with mankind turning its back on God and trying to be god, what are the basic problems created? Can you see these problems playing out in your own life and the lives of others? Give examples.

* Abraham Kuyper, *A Centennial Reader*, edited by James D. Bratt (Grand Rapids, Mich.: Eerdmans, 1998), 488.

One of the problems created by the fall is that everyone in the world views the world differently. In this course we are referring to this as a person's "worldview." Everyone has a basic view of how the world works, but few people have a worldview that is internally consistent, carefully considered, or constantly adhered to. Most people have pieced their worldview together from a variety of experiences and sources.

All worldviews embody some truth and have roots in reality; otherwise, they would not be believable or useful for their adherents. Because many of them also have some overlap with Christianity, it is quite possible for Christians to be taken in by them. We may subscribe to Christian beliefs, but in our workplaces or personal lives operate out of a worldview of, for example, individualism or materialism.

As we seek to live, work and engage culture, we find ourselves confronted with many ways of viewing the world, many systems of belief, and many faiths. If we want to live and work in the world according to a Christian view of the world as revealed in the Bible, it is helpful to learn to discern the alternate worldviews that dominate our culture and our workplaces.

Read the following which will help you start to think through some of these issues.

Understanding worldviews

One of the ways to grasp the concept of a "worldview" is to think of it as a "story." Like every story, it contains:

- A **purpose**, a "mission"—some movement toward a goal that is good and meaningful.

- A **problem** that needs to be resolved to accomplish the goal, or some barrier to be broken through.

- A **solution** to the problem.

A "worldview" is therefore the story of the world that operates at the root of a person's life. It is that person's answer to these questions:

- What is the **purpose** of life or the universe?

  What is the universe all about? Why is there something rather than nothing? Why are we here? What are the main things we should be doing or living for? What is "the goal"?

- What is the **problem** with human nature?

  Why are things not the way they should be? What is the main thing wrong with us? Why aren't we realizing our purpose? Who are the antagonists, or what are the forces hindering us?

- What is the **solution**?

  What is the main way to resolve or fix what is wrong? How can we break through the barrier? Who are the people or what are the forces that will help save us?

Everyone has some kind of worldview that they use to answer these questions.

Six worldviews have been organized in the three clusters on pages 92–94. Each cluster contains worldviews which share a similar view of the purpose of the universe, although they may diverge in their views of the main problem and the solution. Trying to represent any worldview in a few lines means that what follows is reductionistic and an oversimplification. It is not intended to give a comprehensive presentation of these worldviews, but only to convey a very general sense of how to begin to think about worldviews.

The first cluster is the **traditional religious cluster**.

Platonism

- The **purpose**

  The physical world is shadowy and flawed, but the real world is the non-material realm of "Forms" and ideals. The purpose of life is to know and live in accord with the perfect realm of ideals.

- The **problem**

  The soul is good, but the body is bad. Even within the soul, the emotions and desires (tied greatly to the bodily desires for comfort, food, sex) often war against the reason, which, if it is properly educated, is fixed on the realm of the "Forms." The problem is that the body and its passions too often win over reason.

- The **solution**

  We must educate people so that reason triumphs over their bodies and appetites. We must put the most educated citizens, for example the philosophers, in charge of society.

Many traditional religions

- The **purpose**

  There are two worlds, the eternal and the temporal, and this temporal world is the less important. Our purpose is to live a good, moral life and to prepare for eternity.

- The **problem**

  Our problem is moral failure and lack of virtue. Because we do not live the good lives we should, the world has problems.

- The **solution**

  With divine help and the help of the religious community, we make our greatest moral effort to become good and virtuous people who love our families and help the world. This will prepare us for the next world.

Home Study to prepare for Session 6

The second cluster is the **naturalistic cluster.**

Scientific Naturalism

- The **purpose**

  History is a linear movement linked by cause and effect. There is no reality beyond the physical. Everything is the product of biological evolution by means of natural selection. Everything about us is there because it helped us survive. That is the "purpose" of life—to survive.

- The **problem**

  The problems of the world are basically due to competition that produces winners and losers.

- The **solution**

  Empirical investigation and scientific implementation can eliminate many human problems, and in the end the process of evolution moves us "ahead."

Psychodynamism (a catch-all phrase for contemporary individualistic psychology growing out of Freud)

- The **purpose**

  Though this view assumes the scientific worldview of naturalism, it also has roots in Romanticism, which stressed the purpose of individual freedom and discovering our inner self and passion.

- The **problem**

  Human beings are made up of basic primal desires for pleasure and an understanding that these desires must be limited to live in society. Unloving, repressive families and societies are to blame for the imbalance between desires and the conscience, and between the individual and society.

- The **solution**

  Becoming conscious of our true desires, and fulfilling them as much as possible, short of infringing on the freedom of others to do the same.

The third cluster is the **anti-realism cluster.**

Existentialism

- The **purpose**

We are not determined by biological, historical, or economic forces. There are no absolute or objective values or "given" purpose in life, so we are radically free. The purpose of life is to grasp our freedom.

- The **problem**

The problem is that we have to decide who we want to be and how we want to live. We cannot look to tradition to discover this. We must create it completely.

- The **solution**

The solution is to accept our radical freedom and create meaning by fighting meaninglessness—by resisting disease, suffering, sadness, poverty, etc.

Post-modernism

- The **purpose**

Objective knowledge of the "real" world is unachievable. Properties of objects are creative human projections. This agrees with existentialism that we are free to create our own reality, but it says we cannot do this as individuals. All "truth" is socially constructed in communities.

- The **problem**

Community identity unavoidably defines itself by those who are "not-us" or "the other." This marginalizes and oppresses. All truth-claims are really just power plays by one group or another.

- The **solution**

To undermine and deconstruct all truth-claims by unmasking them as socially constructed efforts to maintain power.

Home Study to prepare for Session 6

The Christian worldview

The Christian gospel

- The **purpose**

  God made a good, beautiful world filled with beings to share in this life of joy and peace by knowing, serving, and loving God and one another.

- The **problem**

  Instead, we chose to center our lives on ourselves and on the pursuit of things, rather than on God and others. This led to the disintegration of creation and the loss of peace within ourselves, between people, and in nature itself.

- The **solution**

  God entered history in the person of Jesus to deal with all the causes and results of our broken relationship with him. Jesus lived the life we were created to live and then died to pay the debt of sin incurred for the life we actually live. By his resurrection he showed that death is now defeated and he showed us the future—new bodies and a completely new heaven and new earth, in which the world is restored to full joy, glory, and peace.

	Traditional Religious Cluster	Naturalistic Cluster	Anti-Realism Cluster	Christian Gospel
Purpose	Moral goodness	Survival	Freedom	Knowing God
Problem	Moral failure	Lack of adaptability	Oppression	Sin
Solution	Self (effort)	Self (knowledge)	Self (liberation)	Christ and his grace

The new community required by the Bible cuts across all cultures and worldviews. Put another way: it doesn't fit any worldview but challenges them all at some point. When the gospel "enters" a culture or worldview, it therefore both challenges and affirms; it both retains and rejects. When it enters any culture, it resolves and completes its partly-true story through the gospel.

Lamin Sanneh in *Translating the Message*[2] insists that only Christianity does not decimate an indigenous culture's story, but rather (a) enters it, (b) cleanses it of distortions and idolatrous elements, and (c) resolves its unresolved story lines in Christ.

Select one or two of the worldviews described above and answer the following questions.

1. How is the worldview partly true?

2. How does the gospel cleanse and resolve its story?

We cannot help but participate in the worldview of our particular culture and generation. But the gospel changes the way we look at everything. We are to look at everything, including our work, and decide (a) what to keep as good, (b) what to reject as just too distorted, and (c) what to revise, rename, and reshape with the gospel.

Attempt to answer the questions on the following worksheet to help you think about these issues for your particular workplace.

Questions	In your workplace
What is the main purpose of the work? What goal does it seek to fulfil?	
What methods does it use to achieve its purpose? How does it try to meet the goal?	
Who decides what happens in your workplace? What kinds of people decide what is valued?	
What people or situations influence the decisions that are made?	
What does it mean to be successful?	
What are the idols?	
Whom do people admire?	
How are Christians characterized?	
What about being a Christian is most offensive? What is most acceptable/valued?	
What worldview is predominant in the field or among those in your workplace?	
How does that worldview affect the form and content of the work?	
What parts of the dominant worldview are basically in line with the gospel?	
What parts of the dominant worldview are irresolvable without Christ?	
How can Christ finish the story?	
In what areas do you feel called to challenge your work's culture?	
What opportunities are there to work with excellence and with Christian distinctiveness?	
What opportunities are there for (a) serving people, (b) helping society, (c) witnessing to Christ?	

[2] Lamin Sanneh, *Translating the Message: The Missionary Impact on Culture* (New York: Orbis Books, 1989).

Having completed the worksheet, it would be helpful, if possible, to meet with others in your field to think through the implications.

N.T. Wright in *The Challenge of Jesus* urges us to be at the leading edge of our culture. He writes,

> The gospel of Jesus points us and indeed urges us to be at the leading edge of the whole culture, articulating in story and music and art and philosophy and education and poetry and politics and theology…a worldview that will mount the historically rooted Christian challenge to both modernity and postmodernity, leading the way into the post-postmodern world with joy and humor and gentleness and good judgment and true wisdom. I believe we face the question: if not now, then when? And if we are grasped by this vision, we may also hear the question: if not us, then who? And if the gospel of Jesus is not the key to this task, then what is?"[3]

Pray about the answers you have given and how you, and those in your community, can start to live out your faith at work and be "at the leading edge of the whole culture."

Additional Reading

See **gospelinlife.com** for recommended resources to help you further explore this topic.

98   [3] N.T. Wright, *The Challenge of Jesus* (Downer's Grove, Ill.: IVP, 1999), 196.

Session 6 Work Cultivating The Garden

Summary Of The Previous Session

[*Pray as you begin, asking God to be at work in the group.*]

[*Read the paragraphs below aloud to summarize the main points of the previous session.*]

Last session, we saw that our community is to be a "city on a hill" (Matt. 5:14). The world must see in our community what life can be in all its beauty under the kingship of Jesus Christ.

We also saw that it is important to have gospel-speaking, neighborhood-loving, community-transformed congregations everywhere. Only the gospel enables us to build an alternate city together.

This session's theme is the gospel and our work.

[*Take 3 to 5 minutes to briefly discuss the* Home Study *on pages 88–98. Mention anything you found helpful, new, exciting, or confusing.*]

Bible Study

[*Read aloud Matthew 6:19–21 and then work through the questions below.*]

1. Why does Jesus tell us to store up "treasures in heaven" (v. 20) rather than "treasures on earth" (v. 19)? What does Jesus mean when he says, "For where your treasure is, there your heart will be also"?

2. How do most people you know tend to spend their time, energy, and money? What do you spend money on most effortlessly and joyfully?

3. How might you and your group go about storing up "treasures in heaven"?

4. One way to ensure that we store up treasures in heaven is to celebrate, reflect on, and give thanks for our treasures on earth. This is part of what we do on the Sabbath. In an article called "Bring Back the Sabbath" in *The New York Times Magazine* we read,

   There is ample evidence that our relationship to work is out of whack. Let me argue on behalf of an institution that has kept workaholism in reasonable check for thousands of years. Most people mistakenly believe that all you have to do to stop working is not work. The inventors of the Sabbath understood that it was a much more complicated undertaking. You cannot downshift casually and easily. This is why the Puritan and Jewish Sabbaths were so exactingly intentional. The rules did not exist to torture the faithful. Interrupting the ceaseless round of striving requires a surprisingly strenuous act of will, one that has to be bolstered by habit as well as by social sanction.[1]

This quote explains that scheduled rest will not work without a great deal of intentionality and discipline. Brainstorm the kind of practical habits and useful practices that can help us observe Sabbath.

[*Watch the DVD for Session 6.*]

DVD Notes

[*Use this space if you would like to make notes.*]

[1] J. Shulevitz, "Bring Back the Sabbath" *New York Times Magazine* (March 2, 2003).

Discussion Questions

1. Was there anything from the DVD that was new to you, or had an effect on you? Did you hear anything that raised more questions in your mind?

2. What are some of the practical implications of the biblical teachings that work is good and has dignity?

3. What are some of the practical implications of the biblical teachings that we must not separate God from our work?

4. Besides telling coworkers about Christ, what does it mean to "bring the gospel into your work"? Brainstorm some ways that you can work with Christian distinctiveness in your workplace.

5. In Matthew 11, Jesus promises to "give us rest" (v. 28). How can the deep rest Jesus gives us in the gospel change our relationship to our work?

6. "Do you see your workplace as a place to share the gospel as well as a place to let the gospel shape how you work"? What can you bring into your profession that is uniquely helpful?

Prayer

Thank God that "…there is not a square inch in the whole domain of our human existence over which Christ, who is Sovereign over all, does not cry: 'Mine!'" Ask God to show you ways in which you don't represent Christ as you should in your relationships, in your workplace, in your family life, in your habits and attitudes, and in your relationships within the church. Pray also that you would be able, again within community, to learn better how to "bring the gospel into your work."

Session 6 Work Cultivating The Garden

Introduction Of The Home Study

Session 7 looks at how we relate to our neighbors and our neighborhood. There are many ways to donate our time, money, energy, and effort to help our neighbors. For this *Home Study* you will want to arrange as a group to volunteer at some form of justice or mercy ministry.

Your church leadership should be able to provide you with a list of volunteer opportunities at organizations they know or with which they are associated. Below are some additional volunteer ministry possibilities:

- Ministries that serve the homeless through, for example, meals, food pantries, clothing closets, shelter, medical services, crisis counseling, or job training.
- Ministries that address the special needs of the unemployed, at-risk youth, immigrants, and those without social or family support.
- Ministries that work with youth, adults, and families whose lives have been affected by drug addiction and other serious life-controlling problems.
- Ministries that focus on community issues, such as affordable housing, employment, education, economic development, and health care.
- Ministries that offer education, mentoring, and recreation programs for youth.
- Ministries that give support at special times of the year (e.g., Christmas) by providing gifts and food.

Decide how your group would like to volunteer. Set a definite date and time to serve together. Nominate a member of the group to be in charge of contacting the organization and arranging for everyone to attend. (If it is too difficult for the whole group to find a time to do this together, consider splitting the group into pairs, for example.)

Pray specifically that you would have the heart and find the time to serve the poor and marginalized in the ministry you have chosen.

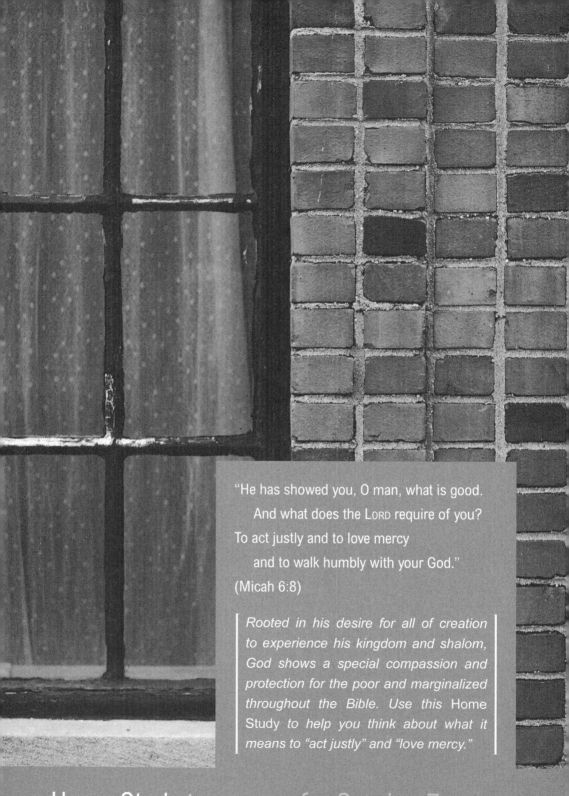

"He has showed you, O man, what is good.
    And what does the LORD require of you?
To act justly and to love mercy
    and to walk humbly with your God."
(Micah 6:8)

Rooted in his desire for all of creation to experience his kingdom and shalom, God shows a special compassion and protection for the poor and marginalized throughout the Bible. Use this Home Study *to help you think about what it means to "act justly" and "love mercy."*

Home Study to prepare for Session 7

The gospel and our neighbor

[*Read the following extract from* Ministries of Mercy[1] *by Timothy Keller.*]

There are two powerful effects that the gospel of grace has on a person who has been touched by it. First, the person who knows that he received mercy while an undeserving enemy of God will have a heart of love for even (and especially!) the most ungrateful and difficult persons. When a Christian sees prostitutes, alcoholics, prisoners, drug addicts, unwed mothers, the homeless, the refugees, he knows that he is looking in a mirror. Perhaps the Christian spent all of his life as a respectable middle-class person. No matter. He thinks: "Spiritually I was just like these people, though physically and socially I never was where they are now. They are outcasts. I was an outcast."

Many people today are very concerned that relief only go to the "deserving" poor. It is true that we must be sure our aid helps a person to self-sufficiency. It is also true that we are not obligated to care for the poor of the world to the same degree that we are bound to help our needy Christian brother. However, we must be very careful about using the word "deserving" when it comes to mercy. Were we ever deserving of God's mercy? If someone is completely deserving, is our aid, then, really mercy?

Years ago, Jonathan Edwards wrote a tract to answer the objections of people to the duty of Christian charity. One objection was, "Why should I help a person who brought himself to his poverty through his own sin?" Edwards responded:

"If they are come [into poverty] by a vicious idleness and prodigality [laziness and self-indulgence]; yet we are not thereby excused from all obligation to relieve them, unless they continue in those vices… If we do otherwise, we shall act in a manner very contrary to the rule of loving one another as Christ loved us. Now Christ hath loved us, pitied us, and greatly laid out himself to relieve us from that want and misery which we brought on ourselves by our own folly and wickedness. We foolishly and perversely threw away those riches with which we were provided, upon which we might have lived and been happy to all eternity."

Clearly, Christians who understand grace will not be quick to give up on an "undeserving" needy person. Christ's mercy was not based on worthiness; it was

[1] Timothy J. Keller, *Ministries of Mercy* (Phillipsburg, N.J.: P&R Publishing, 1989), 60–63.

given to make us worthy. So also our mercy must not only be given to those who reach some standard of worthiness.

Nowhere is this principle stated more starkly than in Luke 6:32–36. Jesus speaks here of loving one's enemies. He is very specific that this love should take the form of action: we must lend to them when they are in need (vv. 33–34) and we must "do good" to them (vv. 33, 35). "Then…you will be sons of the Most High, because he is kind to the ungrateful and wicked. Be merciful, just as your Father is merciful" (vv. 35b–36). God gives mercy to the ungrateful and the wicked—that is what we were. So shall we be like our Father in heaven if we show mercy even to these.

A parable that makes this principle even more forceful is told by Jesus in Matthew 18:21–35. Jesus speaks of a king who forgave a servant a debt of 10,000 talents. Since a talent represented more than a decade and a half of wages for the ordinary worker, it is obvious that Jesus uses this figure to convey the idea of an infinite sum, a debt impossible to pay. After the servant is forgiven, he comes upon a second servant who owes him a small amount of money. The second servant pleads for leniency as the first man had done with the king, but his pleas fall on deaf ears. When the king finally hears of this, he turns to the servant he forgave and says in a rage: "Shouldn't you have had mercy on your fellow servant just as I had on you?" (Matt. 18:33). Jesus' purpose in the parable is to teach the principle of unconditional forgiveness (vv. 22, 35). The ministry of mercy has the same motivation and rationale—the grace of God.

Now we are in a position to see why Jesus (and Isaiah, James, John, and Paul) can use the ministry of mercy as a way to judge between true and false Christianity. A merely religious person, who believes God will favor him because of his morality and respectability, will ordinarily have contempt for the outcast. "I worked hard to get where I am, and so can anyone else!" That is the language of the moralist's heart. "I am only where I am by the sheer and unmerited mercy of God. I am completely equal with all other people." That is the language of the Christian's heart. A sensitive social conscience and a life poured out in deeds of mercy to the needy is the inevitable sign of a person who has grasped the doctrine of God's grace.

Home Study to prepare for Session 7

The second major effect that the gospel of grace has on a person is that it creates spontaneous generosity. The priest and the Levite did not stop despite many biblical injunctions to help a countryman. But no one expects the Samaritan to give mercy. One of the reasons that Jesus puts a Samaritan in the story is that he, by virtue of his race and history, has no obligations at all to stop and give aid. No law, no social convention, no religious prescription dictates that he render service. Yet he stops. Why? Verse 33 [of Luke 10] tells us he was moved by his compassion.

What a clear message! As Edmund Clowney has put it, "God requires the love that cannot be required." Mercy is commanded, but it must not be the response to a command, it is an overflowing generosity as a response to the mercy of God which we received.

Often books and speakers tell Christians that they should help the needy because they have so much. That is, of course, quite true. Common sense tells us that, if human beings are to live together on the planet, there should be a constant sharing of resources.

But this approach is very limited in its motivating power. Ultimately it produces guilt. It says, "How selfish you are to eat steak and drive two cars when the rest of the world is starving!" This creates great emotional conflicts in the hearts of Christians who hear such arguing. We feel guilty, but all sorts of defense mechanisms are engaged. "Can I help it I was born in this country? How will it really help anyone if I stop driving two cars? Don't I have a right to enjoy the fruits of my labor?" Soon, with an anxious weariness, we turn away from books or speakers who simply make us feel guilty about the needy.

The Bible does not use the guilt-producing motivation, yet it powerfully argues for the ministry of mercy. In 2 Corinthians 8:2–3, Paul tells us that the Macedonian Christians gave generously to the Jerusalem famine victims. He notes that "out of the most severe trial, their overflowing joy and their extreme poverty welled up in rich generosity" (v. 2). The Macedonians were not of a higher social class than the needy in Jerusalem. They apparently were going through terrible trials of their own. What, then, was the dynamic that moved them to give? "Their overflowing joy…" (v. 2) and "they gave themselves first to the Lord" (v. 5). It was the Macedonians' response to the self-emptying Lord. Their gifts were a response, not to a ratio of income levels, but to the gift of Christ!

Mercy is spontaneous, superabounding love which comes from an experience of the grace of God. The deeper the experience of the free grace of God, the more generous we must become. This is why Robert Murray M'Cheyne could say: "There are many hearing me who now know well that they are not Christians because they do not love to give. To give largely and liberally, not grudging at all, requires a new heart."

Put another way, the ministry of mercy is a sacrifice of praise to God's grace. The risen Lord of our salvation is not here bodily for us to anoint his feet, but we have the poor to serve as a sacrifice to Christ of love and honor (see John 12:1–8). The offering of the Macedonian believers to the hungry abounds to God in praise (2 Cor. 9:12–15), the Philippians' refreshment of Paul is "an acceptable sacrifice, pleasing to God" (Phil. 4:18), and the writer to the Hebrews teaches that economic sharing is a sacrifice of praise (Heb. 13:15–16).

Why is generosity the mark of being a Christian? Imagine a person who is deathly ill. The doctor announces to him that there is a medicine which can certainly cure him. Without it, he has no hope. "However," says the doctor, "it is extremely expensive. You will have to sell your cars, even your home, to buy it. You may not wish to spend so much." The man turns to his doctor and says, "What do my cars mean to me now? What good will my house be? I must have that medicine; it is precious to me. These other things which were so important to me now look pale by comparison to the medicine. They are expendable now. Give me the medicine." The apostle Peter says, "To you who believe…[he] is precious" (1 Peter 2:7). The grace of God makes Christ precious to us, so that our possessions, our money, our time have all become eternally and utterly expendable. They used to be crucial to our happiness. They are not so now.

| *Having read the extract, answer the following questions.* |

1. What is the scriptural motivation for mercy?

2. What things prevent you from being more merciful?

The Bible and our neighbor

From the beginning, the Bible shows that we are to be engaged in mercy to the poor, the marginalized, and the outcasts. Read the following short survey of this topic through the Bible.

Creation and fall

Adam and Eve are told to rule over all creation (Gen. 1:28); however in Genesis 3, we see that sin brought spiritual alienation from God, emotional alienation within, social alienation from each other, and physical alienation from nature. As a result of the fall, humanity is alienated from God, causing guilt and hostility to the knowledge of the Lord. Men and women are alienated from themselves, causing loss of identity and loss of meaning, as well as anxiety and emptiness. People are alienated from other people, causing war, crime, family breakdown, oppression, and injustice. And finally, humanity is alienated from nature itself, causing hunger, sickness, aging, and physical death. God reveals that his redemption will heal all these effects of sin.

Patriarchal period

Abraham's seed (through Joseph) becomes a blessing to the nations by means of a hunger relief program (Gen. 41:53–57). Job, who lived in this period, is aware that God's judgment falls on those who forget the poor: "If I have denied the desires of the poor or let the eyes of the widow grow weary, if I have kept my bread to myself, not sharing it with the fatherless…if I have seen anyone perishing for lack of clothing, or a needy man without a garment, and his heart did not bless me for warming him with the fleece from my sheep, if I have raised my hand against the fatherless, knowing that I had influence in court, then let my arm fall from the shoulder, let it be broken off at the joint. For I dreaded destruction from God, and for fear of his splendor I could not do such things" (Job 31:16–23).

God gave Israel many laws of social responsibility. Kinsmen and neighbors were obligated to give to the poor man until his need was gone (Deut.15:7–10). Tithes were shared among the poor (Deut. 14:28–29). The poor were also to be given supplies (Deut.15:12–15) and land (Lev. 25), so they could become self-sufficient.

Later Israel

The prophets condemned Israel's insensitivity to the poor as covenant breaking. They taught that materialism and ignoring the poor are sins (Amos 2:6–7); whereas, mercy to the poor is evidence of true relationship with God (Isa. 1:10–17).

The ministry of Christ

Jesus proves to John the Baptist that he is the Christ by pointing out that he heals bodies and preaches to the poor (Matt. 11:1–6), even as the prophets said he would (Isa. 61:1–2). Jesus teaches that anyone who has been touched by the grace of God will be helping the needy (Matt. 5:43–6:4). Jesus, in his incarnation, associated with the lowest class of society. He called this "mercy" (Matt. 9:13).

The early church

Following the prophets, the apostles teach that true faith will inevitably show itself through deeds of mercy (James 2:1–17). "This is how we know what love is: Jesus Christ laid down his life for us. And we ought to lay down our lives for our brothers. If anyone has material possessions and sees his brother in need but has no pity on him, how can the love of God be in him?" (1 John 3:16–17). Within the church, wealth is to be shared very generously between rich and poor (2 Cor. 8:13–15). Materialism is still a grievous sin (James 5:1–6).

[*Read Isaiah 58:3–10 and answer the questions below.*]

1. What is the problem with the people's behavior (vv. 3–6)?

2. Within the context, what does it mean to "loose the chains of injustice"?

3. What is the result of doing this justice (vv. 8–10)?

[*Read James 2:1–17 and answer the questions below.*]

1. Do you perceive the scenario James describes in verses 1–7 to be occurring in your life or in your church? If so, in what ways does it manifest itself?

2. James writes, "For whoever keeps the whole law and yet stumbles at just one point is guilty of breaking all of it" (v. 10). What does he mean by this? What impact does he intend for it to have on his readers? How does he intend for them to change their lives as a result of reading these words?

3. What is the connection between verses 12–13 and verses 14–17?

4. What does this passage tell us about God's concern for the poor, and what are the implications for us?

> *There are many ways to "act justly" and "love mercy." At your previous meeting, your group will have decided to volunteer at some form of mercy ministry. As you take up this opportunity, keep in mind other areas that you may consider getting involved with in the future.*

Relief

This is direct aid to meet physical/material/social needs. The good Samaritan provides physical protection, emergency medical treatment, and a rent subsidy for the man he finds beaten and half-dead in the street (Luke 10:29–37). Relief includes helping at temporary shelters or food pantries or clothing closets for the homeless, providing medical services or crisis counseling, and so on.

Development

This is more about what is needed to bring a person or community to self-sufficiency. In the Old Testament, when a slave's debt was erased and he was released, God directed that his former master send him out with grain, tools, and resources for a new, self-sufficient economic life (Deut.15:12–14). Development includes, for example, providing education, job creation and training, housing development and home ownership, and so on in a community.

Reform

This is about changing social conditions and structures that aggravate or cause poverty and dependency. Job tells us that he not only clothed the naked, but he "broke the fangs of the wicked and snatched the victims from their teeth" (Job 29:17). The prophets denounced unfair wages (Jer. 22:13), corrupt business practices (Amos 8:6), legal systems weighted in favor of the rich and influential (Deut. 24:17; Lev. 19:15), and a system of lending capital that gouges the person of modest means (Ex. 22:25–27). Reform includes, for example, working for a particular community to receive better police protection, fairer banking practices, better laws, and so on.

Home Study to prepare for Session 7

1. Who is your neighbor? Make a list of some people or groups that are in need around you.

2. How do you typically view these people or groups? What emotions come to mind?

3. How does your view differ from God's view?

4. How can you be a neighbor to them? Be practical.

Think about ways you will put your faith into action in the area of showing mercy to the poor and marginalized. Pray that you would find the time and the heart to volunteer. Contact other members of your group and encourage them to attend the volunteer opportunity you have chosen.

Additional Reading

See **gospelinlife.com** for recommended resources to help you further explore this topic.

Once you have volunteered, debrief about the experience with your group. The following questions may help you in this process.

1. What were your expectations going into this volunteer opportunity?

2. How did your experience differ from those expectations?

3. What did you learn about yourself, about the people you served, and about what it means to "act justly and to love mercy" (Micah 6:8)?

4. What would it mean for you, specifically, to allow care for the poor and marginalized to become an integral part of your life?

5. What is one goal that you can accomplish in the next month regarding your personal involvement in justice and mercy for the poor and marginalized?

Session 7 Justice A People For Others

Summary Of The Previous Session

[*Pray as you begin, asking God to be at work in the group.*]

[*Read the paragraphs below aloud to summarize the main points of the previous session.*]

Last session we saw that Christian living is a continual process of bringing everything in line with the truth of the gospel. It means that all of our jobs and gifts and skills are to be realigned in light of the mission of the kingdom of Christ.

We saw that the gospel changes the motivation, ethics, and conception of our work. And that we must take the gospel with us to work.

This session's theme is the gospel and our neighbor.

[*Take 3 to 5 minutes to briefly discuss the* Home Study *on pages 106–115. Mention anything you found helpful, new, exciting, or confusing. Take a few minutes to pray and discuss arrangements for the volunteer opportunity you are planning.*]

Bible Study

[Read aloud Luke 10:25–37 and then work through the questions below.]

1. On the basis of Jesus' teaching, who is our neighbor?

2. Shouldn't we help members of our own family and of our own Christian community first?

3. How does Jesus illustrate what the true motive should be for showing mercy to our neighbor?

4. The following quotes are cited by Rodney Stark, a historian and sociologist who studied the reasons why Christianity spread in the Roman Empire. The Greco-Roman world was struck by several huge plagues or epidemics. Stark traces how the Christians' reaction to the plagues differed dramatically from that of those who maintained faith in traditional, polytheistic paganism.

> The impious Galileans [Christians] support not only their poor, but ours as well, everyone can see that our people lack aid from us.
>
> Roman Emperor Julian (around 360 AD)[1]

[During the great epidemic] most of our brother Christians showed unbounded love and loyalty, never sparing themselves... Heedless of danger, they took charge of the sick, attending to their every need and ministering to them in Christ... Many, in nursing and curing others, transferred their death to themselves and died in their stead... The [pagans] behaved in the very opposite way. At the first onset of the disease, they pushed the sufferers away and fled even from their dearest, throwing them into the roads before they were dead.

Dionysius, Bishop of Alexandria (around 260 AD)[2]

Having read these quotes, what is the effect of unselfish service on others? Have you found this to be true in your own experience? Give examples.

[*Watch the DVD for Session 7.*]

DVD Notes

[*Use this space if you would like to make notes.*]

[1] Quoted in Rodney Stark, *The Rise of Christianity* (San Francisco: Harper, 1997), 84. [2] Ibid., 82–83.

Discussion Questions

1. Was there anything from the DVD that was new to you, or had an effect on you? Did you hear anything that raised more questions in your mind?

2. "*Shalom* means total flourishing in absolutely every dimension: physically, relationally, socially, and spiritually." In what practical ways can you and your group "resolve to have shalom felt everywhere…and begin to reweave the broken fabric of creation"? What can you as a group (or a church) bring into your neighborhood that is uniquely helpful?

3. Benjamin Fernando from Sri Lanka writes,

> There is no such thing as a separate individual gospel and a separate social gospel. There is only one gospel—a redeemed man in a reformed society… Social problems assume greater importance in Christianity than in Buddhism or Hinduism. The theory of Karma and rebirth gives a fairly reasonable explanation for social inequalities of this life which on the one hand are consequences of

the previous life and on the other hand can be compensated for in the next life. But to a Christian there is only one earthly life and so social problems have to be dealt with now or never.[3]

Do you agree with his assessment that "social problems have to be dealt with now or never"? Why or why not?

4. The Bible reveals at least three causal factors for poverty: injustice and oppression; circumstantial calamity; and personal failure. Do you agree? Can you give examples of these from the Bible or from your own experience?

5. "It's natural to want to help people who are like you, who like you, and who you like." What would it mean for you, specifically, to help people who are not like you, who do not like you, and who you do not like?

---

[3] Benjamin E. Fernando, "The Evangel and Social Upheaval (part 2)", in *Christ Seeks Asia*, ed. W.S. Mooneyham (Charlestown, Ind.: Rock House, 1969), 118–119.

6. Jonathan Edwards once was preaching on how important it was to give to the poor. Someone later objected, "I can't afford to give to the poor." Edwards responded with an application of Galatians 6:2.

> In many cases, we may, by the rules of the gospel, be obliged to give to others, when we cannot do it without suffering ourselves… If our neighbor's difficulties and necessities be much greater than our own, and we see that he is not like to be otherwise relieved, we should be willing to suffer with him, and to take part of his burden on ourselves; else how is that rule of bearing one another's burdens fulfilled? If we are never obliged to relieve others' burdens, but when we can do it without burdening ourselves, then how do we bear our neighbor's burdens, when we bear no burden at all?[4]

Do you agree that we are not only to help others with our excess time, money, and emotional resources, but that we are to give until it burdens us? What will this mean for you and your group?

[4] Jonathan Edwards, *The Works of Jonathan Edwards* (Edinburgh: Banner of Truth, 1834), Volume 2, 171.

Prayer

"Justice is the index of real faith, the index of a real relationship with God—of the real spiritual condition of your heart." Confess fears, weaknesses, and indifference to all those Jesus would identify as your neighbors. Pray for the poor, and pray as well that you and your community would help the poor and marginalized, even when it is risky and costly to you.

Introduction Of The Home Study

To introduce you to the final session of the course, the *Home Study* focuses on the earthly city and the heavenly city; our home now and our heavenly home; the world that is and the world that is to come.

"This is what the LORD Almighty, the God of Israel, says to all those I carried into exile from Jerusalem to Babylon: 'Build houses and settle down; plant gardens and eat what they produce. Marry and have sons and daughters; find wives for your sons and give your daughters in marriage, so that they too may have sons and daughters. Increase in number there; do not decrease. Also, seek the peace and prosperity of the city to which I have carried you into exile. Pray to the LORD for it, because if it prospers, you too will prosper.'" (Jeremiah 29:4–7)

The quote above describes how God wanted the people of Israel to conduct themselves in the pagan city and culture where they found themselves living. Use this Home Study *to contemplate the earthly city and the heavenly city, the world that is and the world that is to come.*

Home Study to prepare for Session 8

Living in the world that is

In the history of Israel covered by the Bible, there were periods during which the Israelites lived as believers in a pluralistic, pagan environment among people with vastly different worldviews. For example, when they reached Canaan, they failed to drive out the idol-worshiping people and, instead, settled in among them. Also, when Nebuchadnezzar defeated Jerusalem, he carried most of the Israelites off to live in the city and environs of Babylon. In both situations, believers did not live in a believing culture, where the government, the arts, and the cultural institutions were committed to the Lord and his Word and will. They lived in an environment where the dominant culture was pagan and the dominant worldview dissimilar to their own.

There are many ways Christians can relate to and live in an unbelieving, dominant culture. Read the following to help you think through them. (Please note that the "attitudes" below are not perfectly distinct categories.)

Attitude 1—assimilating the city

Christians simply give in and adopt the pagan culture's values and worldview. The goal is to blend in and lose any distinct identity. Judges gives us many examples of this. By the time of Samson (Judg. 14–16), the Israelites were so accommodated to Philistine culture that they were within a generation of losing all distinct identity.

Attitude 2—reflecting the city

Christians keep some aspects of Christian faith and practice, but they adopt the more fundamental values and worldviews of the dominant culture. Faith is for Sunday services and does not shape the way they actually live. Their lifestyle is fundamentally no different from those around them. Thus they are just a subset of the dominant culture. The story of Micah and his mother in Judges 17–18 is a great example.

Attitude 3—despising the city

Christians respond to the prevailing culture with superiority and hostility. They feel polluted by the presence of the unbelieving schools, entertainment, and arts. Some take a more passive approach and withdraw from any real interaction, just denouncing and bewailing the moral decay, while others aim to acquire cultural power. Psalm 137 gives us a picture of people who are more angry than repentant over their new powerless situation, and who cannot envision how they can worship outside of the land where they had sovereignty.

Attitude 4—ignoring the city

Christians respond not with too much pessimism but too much optimism. They expect a miraculous, sweeping intervention by God, which will convert many or most and explosively transform the culture. Consequently, instead of becoming deeply engaged with the society and people around them, working with others to help with the troubles and problems, Christians concentrate completely on building up the church and their own numbers. Christians are pressed to go into ministry but not to become playwrights, artists, lawyers, or business people. They are just "passing through," and not becoming involved. The prophet Hananiah in Jeremiah 28 is a great example of this kind of approach.

Attitude 5—loving the city

Christians engage with the dominant culture, but in ways that reveal the distinctiveness of the values of the kingdom of God. They are at their core very different in the way they understand money, relationships, human life, sex, and so on. Christians are truly residents of the city, yet not seeking power over or the approval of the dominant culture. Rather, they show the world an alternative way of living and of being a human community. For example, they are actively involved in serving those around them and in deeds of mercy and justice. Jeremiah's letter to the exiles in chapter 29 is a good example of this.

Note

Today, a city is typically defined almost exclusively in terms of population size. Larger population centers are called "cities," smaller ones "towns," and the smallest are "villages." However, the main Hebrew word for city, 'iyr, means any human settlement surrounded by some fortification or wall. Most ancient cities numbered only about 1,000–3,000 in population.

[*Answer the following questions.*]

1. Which attitude do people you know generally take, and why?

2. Consider Attitude 5. How can you and your group stand out from the prevailing culture in the way you understand money, relationships, sex, and human life?

3. Harvie Conn writes:

> Perhaps the best analogy to describe all this is that of a model home... On a tract of earth's land purchased with the blood of Christ, Jesus the kingdom developer has begun building new housing. As a sample of what will be, he has erected a model home of what will eventually fill the urban neighborhood. Now he invites the...world into that model home to take a look at what will be. The church is the occupant of that model home, inviting neighbors into its open door to Christ. Evangelism is when the signs are put up saying, "Come in and look around"... In this model home we live out our new lifestyle as citizens of the heavenly city that one day will come. We do not abandon our jobs or desert the city that is... We are...to "seek the peace and prosperity of the city to which" God carried us in exile (Jer. 29: 7).[1]

Is your church community a model home, as described by the quote above? What can you and your group do to make this increasingly the case?

[1] Harvie Conn, *Planting and Growing Urban Churches* (Grand Rapids, Mich.: Baker, 1997), 202.

The Bible and the city

The Bible denounces many cities as places of violence, oppression, and unbelief. The prophets in particular denounced the urban life of Israel (e.g., Micah 3:9–11: "Hear this…you rulers of the house of Israel, who despise justice and distort all that is right; who build Zion with bloodshed, and Jerusalem with wickedness. Her leaders judge for a bribe…and her prophets tell fortunes for money").

It is, however, only because the Bible assumes the city is something good, something which God has made, that the denunciations are so vehement. The Bible's attitude is never, "It's the city, so what do you expect?" but rather, "Cities aren't supposed to be like this." Cities are now broken by sin, just as families and churches are. But we don't discard family life—we seek to renew and restore it by God's grace. The same should be true for cities.

The below is a short overview of the importance of "the city" in the Bible. Read through it and think about how you view the city.

Creation and fall

God tells Adam and Eve to "rule over" (Gen. 1:28) the earth, to bring forth the riches God put in nature (and human nature) at creation. This is a call to engage in the arts, science, enterprise, family life. God intends for Adam and Eve to build a city, but Adam and Eve soon fail their commission to be servants of God and to cultivate creation under his lordship.

The occupation of Canaan

When God settles the Israelites in Canaan, he commands them to build "cities of refuge, to which a person who has killed someone accidentally may flee. They will be places of refuge from the avenger, so that a person accused of murder may not die before he stands trial before the assembly" (Num. 35:11–12). God commands the building of cities, because cities with walls and with a gathered population can protect an accused man and provide a trial for him in a way that rural areas can't.

Home Study to prepare for Session 8

David's kingdom

David is directed by God to establish his house in the midst of a city—Jerusalem—which becomes a sign and symbol of the future city of God. When Israel makes Jerusalem its capital, God directs that the temple be built on Mount Zion so it will rise above the city as its "skyscraper," but unlike skyscrapers designed for their builders' own prosperity (e.g., the skyscraper of Babel built to "make a name for ourselves" in Genesis 11:4). God's city is different: "In the city of our God, his holy mountain…is beautiful in its loftiness, the joy of the whole earth" (Ps. 48:1–2).

The exile

God calls the Jewish exiles to "seek the peace and prosperity" of the pagan city of Babylon, to which they had been taken captive. They are to serve the common good of the city and to pray for it (Jer. 29:7).

The Wisdom Literature

Proverbs 11:10–11 reflects the situation of the people of God living in a pagan city:

> When the righteous prosper, the city rejoices;
>> when the wicked perish, there are shouts of joy.
> Through the blessing of the upright a city is exalted,
>> but by the mouth of the wicked it is destroyed.

Proverbs 11:10 speaks of "the righteous" as a discrete grouping within the city. This seems to rule out the idea that the writer is thinking of Jerusalem or some other Israelite city. He says that God's people within the city are to "prosper" as a way to benefit the city.

The teaching and work of Jesus

The call to build Jerusalem and the call to the exiles to seek the peace of Babylon are both important backdrops to Jesus' call that his followers be a "city on a hill" (Matt. 5:14). Jesus calls his disciples to be God's urban alternative—to form an alternate city within the city—that is visible to all (on a hill).

Jesus travels to the great city, Jerusalem, to make his sacrifice for sin. The book of Hebrews tells us, "The high priest carries the blood of animals into the Most Holy Place as a sin offering, but the bodies are burned outside the camp. And so Jesus also suffered outside the city gate to make the people holy through his own blood" (Heb. 13:11–12).

The ministry of Paul

In Acts 17 Paul goes to Athens, the intellectual center of the Greco-Roman world, and then in Acts 18 to Corinth, one of the commercial centers of the empire, and then in Acts 19 to Ephesus, often seen as the religious center of the Roman world. Paul by the end of the book of Acts makes it to Rome, which was the military and political center of that world. In his commentary on the book of Acts, John Stott concludes, "It seems to have been Paul's deliberate policy to move purposefully from one strategic city-centre to the next."[2]

The Epistles

Both James and Peter begin their epistles by calling Christians "scattered" among the nations (James 1:1; 1 Peter 1:1). The key metaphor that 1 Peter employs to express the Christians' relationship to the city around them is that of "resident aliens" (*paroikos; parepidemos*)—people who are neither transient (or hostile) to the host country, nor assimilated into it. They are permanent residents of a new country they love. On the other hand, they differ significantly in their way of life; they are aliens.

The consummation

In Revelation 21–22, we catch a glimpse of the climax of history, when the world is finally in the condition Jesus died to produce. We discover that in the world that is to come the earth has become a city. This final city will have all the superlative greatness of city life without any of its blemishes, weaknesses, and flaws under sin. Our destination is not a return ticket to the garden of Eden, but entry into "the Holy City, the new Jerusalem" (Rev. 21:2). God begins history in a garden, but he ends it in a city!

Home Study to prepare for Session 8

Calvin, Luther, and Edwards on the world that is to come

[*Read the extracts below describing the world that is to come.*]

Calvin writes, in his *Institutes of the Christian Religion*:

> Christ, the Sun of Righteousness [Mal. 4:2], shining through the gospel and having overcome death, has, as Paul testifies, brought us the light of life [II Tim. 1:10]. Hence we likewise by believing "pass out of death into life" [John 5:24], being "no more strangers and sojourners, but fellow citizens of the saints and of the household of God" [Eph. 2:19], who "made us sit" with his only-begotten Son "in heavenly places" [Eph. 2:6], that we may lack nothing for full happiness... Paul says in another passage that "we have died, and our life is hid with Christ in God. When Christ, who is our life, appears, then we also will appear with him in glory" [Col. 3:3–4]...[3] Let us always have in mind the eternal happiness, the goal of resurrection—a happiness of whose excellence the minutest part would scarce be told if all were said that the tongues of all men can say. For though we very truly hear that the Kingdom of God will be filled with splendor, joy, happiness, and glory, yet when these things are spoken of, they remain utterly remote from our perception, and, as it were, wrapped in obscurities, until that day comes when he will reveal to us his glory, that we may behold it face to face [cf. I Cor. 13:12].[4]

In *The Table Talk of Martin Luther*, Luther writes:

> "God will create a new heaven and a new earth, wherein righteousness shall dwell." It will be no arid waste, but a beautiful new earth, where all the just will dwell together. There will be no carnivorous beasts, or venomous creatures, for all such, like ourselves, will be relieved from the curse of sin... The foliage of the trees, and the verdure of the grass, will have the brilliancy of emeralds; and we ourselves delivered from our mundane subjection to gross appetites and necessities, shall have the same form as here, but infinitely more perfect. Our eyes will be radiant as the purest silver, and we shall be exempt from all sickness and tribulation. We shall behold the glorious Creator face to face.[5]

[2] John Stott, *The Message of Acts* in Bible Speaks Today series (Downers Grove, Ill.: IVP, 1990), 293. [3] John Calvin, *Institutes of the Christian Religion*, Battles Edition, Book 3, Chapter XXV, Section 1 (Louisville: Westminster Press, 1960), 987–988. [4] Ibid., Section 10, pages 1004–1005. [5] Martin Luther, *The Table Talk of Martin Luther*, translated by William Hazlitt (London: Bell & Daldry, 1872), 322–323.

In his sermon *Heaven, a World of Love*, Edwards said:

The most stately cities on earth, however magnificent their buildings, yet have their foundations in the dust, and their streets dirty and defiled, and made to be trodden under foot; but the very streets of this heavenly city are of pure gold, like unto transparent glass, and its foundations are of precious stones, and its gates are pearls... There are many principles contrary to love, that make this world like a tempestuous sea. Selfishness, and envy, and revenge, and jealousy, and kindred passions keep life on earth in a constant tumult... But oh! what rest is there in that world which the God of peace and love fills with his own gracious presence, and in which the Lamb of God lives and reigns, filling it with the brightest and sweetest beams of his love; where there is nothing to disturb or offend, and no being or object to be seen that is not surrounded with perfect amiableness and sweetness...where there is no enemy and no enmity; but perfect love in every heart and to every being; where there is perfect harmony among all the inhabitants, no one envying another, but everyone rejoicing in the happiness of every other... where love is always mutual and reciprocated to the full; where there is no hypocrisy or dissembling, but perfect simplicity and sincerity; where there is no treachery, or unfaithfulness, or inconstancy, or jealousy in any form...where there is no division through different opinions or interests, but where all in that glorious and loving society shall be most nearly and divinely related, and each shall belong to every other, and all shall enjoy each other in perfect prosperity and riches, and honor, without any sickness, or grief, or persecution, or sorrow, or any enemy to molest them, or any busybody to create jealousy or misunderstanding, or mar the perfect, and holy, and blessed peace that reigns in heaven![6]

Home Study to prepare for Session 8

[*Use the following questions to help you think through the extracts.*]

1. **What are the differences and similarities between the three descriptions of the world to come?**

2. **What specific phrases or concepts were striking or helpful to you? Why?**

[*Pray that you would be enabled to live in the perspective that these extracts bring.*]

Additional Reading

See **gospelinlife.com** for recommended resources to help you further explore this topic.

[*Since the next session is the final session of the course, take time to review your notes and answers from the past sessions and then complete the gospel self-assessment questionnaire on the following pages.*]

⁶ From Jonathan Edwards' sermon *Heaven, a World of Love*, source: http://www.biblebb.com/files/edwards/charity16.htm

The purpose of this questionnaire is to help you think about areas you have grown in, areas you could grow in, areas that resonated with you, and why. We encourage you to repeat it on an annual basis to see how you have progressed in these areas.

Pray. Pray for wisdom to have an accurate assessment of yourself.

Think hard. Answer each question honestly after taking time to think about it.

Seek counsel from others. Many of the questions are difficult to answer about yourself. The questionnaire will be most useful to you if you obtain feedback from others by asking them to look over your answers to this questionnaire. Think about asking a close friend or your group leader to reflect on your answers to see if they agree, or if they have anything to add.

Gospel and the heart

1. Do you know God, rely on God, seek God, and praise God genuinely? What practical steps can you take to make this more the case?

2. What does Christ mean in your life on a daily basis? In what areas of your life is Christ having a significant impact? In what areas should he be having greater impact?

Gospel Self-Assessment Questionnaire

3. Are you confident that you are righteous in God's sight? What things tend to make you forget this, or to question this? What things do you rely on other than Christ? What steps can you take to change?

4. What idols are you struggling with? How are you dealing with pride, fear of man, attachment to money, sexual lust, preoccupation with your own performance, and the like?

5. Do you admit your limits, mistakes, sins, and weaknesses to God, others, yourself?

To God:	Never	Seldom	Occasionally	Frequently	Always
To others:	Never	Seldom	Occasionally	Frequently	Always
To yourself:	Never	Seldom	Occasionally	Frequently	Always

6. How have you changed over the past year?

Are you a more loving person than you were last year?
Are you a more joyful person than you were last year? Do you give thanks more?
Are you a more peaceful person? Do you worry less?
Are you more patient? With people? With circumstances?
Are you a kinder person?
Can you take criticism better?
Are you bolder, more courageous, and more confident in following Christ?
Are you a less angry, more gentle person?
Are you a more self-controlled person? In what areas? Where do you still need to change?

1. Are you developing relationships within your church family? Is there a group of Christians in the church with whom you share life, with whom you are transparent, and who feel like family?

2. Are you accountable to a Christian community? Are there areas of your life where you feel you need more accountability? What are they?

3. Do you serve willingly and joyfully? Do you serve yourself or others primarily? Are you doing things out of selfish ambition, or do you put the interests of others first?

4. Are your life and behavior disciplined, consistent, and winsome? Would people want to imitate what they see of your faith, your faithfulness, and your character?

5. Is sharing the gospel a regular part of your life? Are you active in telling others about Christ?

Gospel Self-Assessment Questionnaire

6. How have you changed over the past year?

Do you regularly love and encourage others, even when under stress or undergoing suffering?

Are you more able to love people you do not necessarily like?

Do you regularly communicate love and affection toward others in a visible way?

Do you regularly offer hospitality to those around you?

Are you more able to unselfishly help others with their needs and problems?

Are you better able to challenge and confront others but to do so with love and humility?

Are you regularly helping others to grow and mature in their faith?

Are you a more forgiving person than you were last year?

Are you more involved with the needs of others?

In what ways could you do more?

7. How frequently do you take part in the following?

Individual prayer			
Every day / Almost every day	2–4 times a week	Weekly	Monthly

Group prayer (e.g., with family, in your small group, as part of serving, etc.)			
Every day / Almost every day	2–4 times a week	Weekly	Monthly

Personal Bible reading			
Every day / Almost every day	2–4 times a week	Weekly	Monthly

Group Bible reading (e.g., with family, in your small group, as part of serving, etc.)			
Every day / Almost every day	2–4 times a week	Weekly	Monthly

Are these a regular part of your life? How can they become a more regular part?

1. How often do you give your time to ministries of justice or mercy? In what ways are you involved in the lives of the poor, the marginalized, and the suffering? What motivates you to do this? How can you do more?

2. In what ways do you give of your time, energy, and resources? Do you give significantly, substantially, sacrificially, and willingly? Could you do more?

3. What do you do to practice Sabbath rest? Are you taking time to rest or are you too consumed by your work? How can you rest more effectively?

4. How do you honor Christ in your work or daily tasks? In what ways do you see your work as a restoration of shalom?

5. How often do you pray for the city? Do you seek its "peace and prosperity"? In what ways do you use and abuse the place where you live? In what ways do you love and serve the place where you live?

6. Is there a role or area of service you should take on/continue/stop?

7. Of the three categories "heart," "community," and "world," is there an area you resonate with and want to learn more about?

Pray about the answers you have given, asking the Holy Spirit to be at work in your life.

Session 8 Eternity The World That Is To Come

Summary Of The Previous Session

[*Pray as you begin, asking God to be at work in the group.*]

[*Read the paragraphs below aloud to summarize the main points of the previous session.*]

Last session we saw that we are to bring shalom to the world. We need to "act justly" and "love mercy." We are to be engaged with our neighbors and with the poor and marginalized.

We saw that a deep social conscience and a life poured out in deeds of service to others, and especially to the poor, is the inevitable sign of real faith and a real relationship with God.

In this final session on the course we will be thinking about eternity.

[*Take 3 to 5 minutes to briefly discuss the* Home Study *on pages 124–133. Mention anything you found helpful, new, exciting, or confusing.*]

Bible Study

[*Read aloud Isaiah 60:15–22 and then work through the questions below.*]

1. What will heaven be like according to Isaiah's description in verses 17–21? How does this compare with the description in Revelation 21:1–4, 22–27?

2. How can the knowledge that there will be no violence or destruction in the future kingdom help us, and those we come into contact with, to cope with the violence and destruction we experience around us?

3. God is described in a variety of ways and given a variety of titles in this passage. What do we learn about God and what does it mean for our relationship with him?

4. Richard Mouw writes:

> My own hunch is that God has provided us with a rich storehouse of diverse images of the afterlife, all of them hints in the direction of something that is beyond our present comprehension, so that we can be free to draw on one or another of them as a particular situation in our life may require.[1]

In what situations might we draw on the description of heaven in Isaiah 60? What other descriptions of eternity have you drawn on in the past and why?

[*Read aloud Isaiah 60:1–14 and then* ***watch the DVD for Session 8.***]

DVD Notes

[*Use this space if you would like to make notes.*]

---

[1] Richard J. Mouw, *When the Kings Come Marching In* (Grand Rapids, Mich.: Eerdmans, 2002), x.

Discussion Questions

1. Was there anything from the DVD that was new to you, or had an effect on you? Did you hear anything that raised more questions in your mind?

2. Isaiah 60 describes a vision of the New Jerusalem as incorporating the cultural achievements of all people and all nations. What aspects of your work do you think might be incorporated into this final kingdom? How does this affect your understanding of your work?

3. The community described here is one of perfectly restored shalom. What are some tangible ways that the church can be a better foretaste of that community?

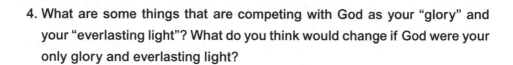

4. What are some things that are competing with God as your "glory" and your "everlasting light"? What do you think would change if God were your only glory and everlasting light?

5. Now that you have completed the gospel in life course, take a few minutes to look back through your notes and then share with the group one thing that changed or affected you, and explain why. Pray about these discoveries and realizations during your time of prayer together.

Prayer

Thank God for the amazing vision we have of the New Jerusalem. Pray that this vision would drive you and your community to action. Ask God to give you insight into his specific kingdom plans and purposes for your city and community. Ask to fit into his plan.

Pray that you would be able to put into practice all you have learned in these eight sessions, and that you would continually seek to transform your heart, community, and the world. Pray for each other in light of your answers to question 5 above.

Assessment

Now that the course is over, think about what areas of service and ministry you could get involved with. Your leader will be scheduling a meeting with you to help you think about your next steps.

In preparation:

- Pray about the things you have learned in this course.

- Be ready to discuss with your leader what you think would most help you to grow and stand firm in your faith—other courses? books to read? practices to put in place?

- Research opportunities your church has for service—talk to your pastor(s) or other church leaders; look at your church website.

- Research ways you could get involved with or support some form of justice and mercy ministry.

- Review (or complete) the worldview workplace exercise on page 97. Write down and pray about some practical things you could do in the next weeks and months.

- Review the gospel self-assessment questionnaire on pages 134–139 and be ready to discuss it with your leader.

gospel[in]life

[Notes for Leaders]

Contents

Introduction Notes for Leaders

How To Use This Guide

This guide includes eight group studies as well as individual *Home Studies*. Each group study consists of:

10 minutes	A summary of the previous session
20 minutes	A Bible study
10 minutes	A DVD presentation by Timothy Keller
25 minutes	Discussion questions about the DVD
5 minutes	An introduction to next session's *Home Study*

Throughout this guide, instructions are in italics and surrounded by these brackets: [ ]

This section contains notes under the questions to help you prepare to lead your group. You will need to read through the notes for each study in advance. These notes are not intended for you to look at during your group study; they are intended as advance preparation. Please use the appropriate pages in the front of this guide during the group study.

You do not need to complete all the questions included in the studies. Set the appropriate time limit for your group and stick to it. An indication of timing was given in the box above.

Depending on the dynamic of the group, you may find that you can only complete three or four questions in the time allocated. If this is the case, review the questions beforehand and choose the ones that will be of most value to your group. You know your group and which questions might be too difficult and/or uninteresting to them. It is important, therefore, to customize and/or choose the questions before you arrive at the study.

Do not spend your entire time allocation on the first question. Try to keep the discussions on topic and moving through the questions you have chosen.

This guide does not prescribe how to run your group. Please use these studies in whatever group or classroom context your church recommends. Please add any additional elements you like, for example singing together, eating together, anything that helps build community.

Home Studies

In the front of this guide, the *Home Studies* are printed on gray pages to distinguish them from the group studies on white pages.

The *Home Studies* consist of a series of readings, quotations, exercises, questions, and projects to help delve deeper into the topic of the next session. It will take about an hour to complete each *Home Study*.

Briefly describe the purpose of the *Home Study* to your group at the end of each group study. Be enthusiastic about the *Home Studies*—if you are eager to complete them, your group will be too.

The *Home Studies* to prepare for Session 5 and Session 7 are projects. You will need to familiarize yourself with these ahead of time in order to have sufficient time to prepare for them.

Acknowledgments

gospelⁱⁿlife was developed from material by Timothy Keller and Redeemer Presbyterian Church by Scott Kauffmann, John Lin, and Sam Shammas.

We are deeply grateful to: Lukas Naugle, Peter Ostebo, and the team at Desiring God for the production of the DVD; Marty McAlpine for the photography; Carl Larsen for the motion graphics; Diane Bainbridge for the Study Guide design; and Greg Clouse, Mike Cook, Robin Phillips, John Raymond, and the rest of the Zondervan team for their continued partnership.

The course has been greatly enhanced by the contributions of Andi Brindley, Abe Cho, Kathy Keller, Katherine Leary, Scott Sauls, Cindy Widmer, the fellowship groups at Redeemer Presbyterian Church, and the many other churches who graciously offered feedback as they piloted the material.

Notes for Leaders

Session 1 City The World That Is

Bible Study Notes For Leaders

In 586 BC, Jerusalem was destroyed and the elite of Jewish society—the artisans and professionals and leaders—were taken to Babylon by force. The prophet Jeremiah received a word from the Lord and wrote these exiles a letter. Read Jeremiah 29:4–14, and then work through the questions and notes below ahead of time to help you prepare to lead your group. The notes beneath the questions are not intended as answers to be read aloud. They are notes to help you facilitate the discussion.

1. **What specific directions does God give the exiles for relating to the city of Babylon in verses 4–7? How do you think the exiles felt about this?**

Settle in the city

They are to "settle down" (v. 5). They are to plan for long-term involvement and invest in the community: "Build houses" and "plant gardens" (v. 5).

Grow in the city

They are to "Increase in number there; do not decrease" (v. 6b). This means they are to get stronger and more numerous, but it also means that they are not to lose their unique identity. They must stand firm in their faith.

Seek the city's peace and prosperity

When Jeremiah says, "Also, seek the peace and prosperity of the city" (v. 7), he means they are to seek their own prosperity in such a way that it benefits the city. They are to use their gifts and resources in such a way that helps the whole city. They are not to use the city for their own advancement, but are to seek its advancement.

Pray for the city

They are to "Pray to the LORD for it" (v. 7b). God calls them to pray for the city.

Note that God's denunciation of the false prophets in verses 8 and 9 comes immediately after the directions in verses 4 through 7 to (a) settle and be involved in the city, and (b) seek its peace. The prophets' advice is contrasted with God's; therefore, we conclude that these false prophets were telling the exiles the opposite of the directions of verses 4 through 7—namely to (a) stay detached and outside the city and (b) remain hostile to it.

To get an idea of what the prophets were promoting, see Jeremiah 28:2–4, where Hananiah prophesies, "Within two years I will bring back to this place all the...exiles from Judah who went to Babylon...for I will break the yoke of the king of Babylon." Jeremiah contradicts this prediction (see Jer. 29:28) and says, "It will be a long time. Therefore build houses and settle down."

2. What is the relationship between the "prosper you" of verse 11 and the "prosperity of the city" of verse 7?

They are cause and effect. When we put verses 11 and 7 together, we see a dynamic principle at work. The believers will find their own peace and prosperity not in seeking their own prosperity, but in seeking the prosperity of the city. It is only as the Jews give up their resentment and scorn of Babylon and seek to serve it and prosper it that, paradoxically, they will find their own prosperity. Verse 7b says it quite directly: "If [Babylon] prospers, you too will prosper." If they concentrate on bringing peace and prosperity *to* this pagan city (v. 7a), God will bring them peace and prosperity *through* this pagan city (v. 7b). God ties, as it were, the fortunes of the people of God to the effectiveness of their urban ministry.

Derek Kidner in his commentary on Jeremiah writes of Jeremiah 29:7, "Even the New Testament, with its instructions to overcome evil with good (Rom. 12:21) and to 'adorn the doctrine of God' by 'perfect courtesy toward all men' (Titus 2:10; 3:2; 1 Peter 2:18), hardly outstrips the boldness of this teaching... To set themselves something to live for, and something to give their captors...was...the surest way—and still is—to the givers' own enrichment, as verse 7b points out."[1]

[1] Derek Kidner, *The Message of Jeremiah* (Downers Grove, Ill.: IVP, 1987), 100.

Ask the group to take a moment to make this personal—i.e., ask the group to come up with personal examples and to apply this to their own life. What is this text in Jeremiah 29:7 saying? That through you, God can bring his peace and prosperity to the city, and through ministry to the city, he will bring his peace and prosperity to you.

3. What was the purpose of the exile, according to verses 11–14? Why do you think these verses were included in the letter?

Three times God spells out that he "carried" the exiles to the city (verses 4, 7, and 14). "Carried" is a very active word—it says far more than that God just "allowed" them to be deported. In other words, their life in the pluralistic city of Babylon is not a senseless disaster—it is part of God's design for them.

Also, God says that he has set times and a schedule for them. He has put them there for seventy years, two or three generations (v. 10). The seventy-year exile allows two things to happen.

First, the seventy years are "for Babylon" (v. 10a) itself. This seems to mean that God had plans for what he wanted to do in the world through Babylon. But, there is another way in which the seventy years are "for" Babylon. When the Jews came to Babylon they, of course, brought their faith in God with them. The Babylonians would therefore be brought into contact with people who believed in the true and living God.

Second, the purpose of the seventy years is for the spiritual purification and renewal of Israel. God's people were in a state of spiritual disintegration (see verses 19 and 23), but the exile would change all that. They will develop a rich life of prayer, according to verse 12: "Then you will call upon me and come and pray to me, and I will listen to you." They will seek fellowship with God in wholehearted openness to him—verses 13–14 say: "You will seek me and find me when you seek me with all your heart. I will be found by you." In fact, God goes so far as to say that the final result of the exile will be to "prosper you and not to harm you" (v. 11).

4. Rodney Stark, a sociologist of religion, writes,

> Christianity served as a revitalization movement that arose in response to the misery, chaos, fear, and brutality of life in the urban Greco-Roman world... Christianity revitalized life in...cities by providing new norms and new kinds of social relationships able to cope with many urgent urban problems. To cities filled with the homeless and impoverished, Christianity offered charity as well as hope. To cities filled with newcomers and strangers, Christianity offered an immediate basis for attachments... To cities torn by violent ethnic strife, Christianity offered a new basis for social solidarity. And to cities faced with epidemics, fires and earthquakes, Christianity offered effective...services.[2]

Is this still true of Christianity today? If not, why not? In what ways does Christianity "revitalize life" in your area?

Discuss with your group.

[*Watch the DVD for Session 1 to help you prepare to lead your group through the discussion that follows.*]

[2] Rodney Stark, *The Rise of Christianity* (New York: Harper, 1997), 161.

Discussion Questions Notes For Leaders

After watching the DVD with your group, use these questions to encourage discussion. The notes beneath the questions are not intended as answers to be read aloud. They are notes to help you facilitate the discussion.

You do not need to complete all the questions. Depending on the dynamic of the group and your time limit, you may find it helpful to choose in advance the questions that will be of most value to your group and start with those.

Remember a city is defined as "any place of density, diversity, and cultural energy."

1. Was there anything from the DVD that was new to you, or had an effect on you? Did you hear anything that raised more questions in your mind?

Discuss with your group.

2. J.N. Manokaran, a pastor from India, writes in his book *Christ and Cities*, "Cities should not be seen as monsters...but communities of people with need."[3] How do you view the place in which you live? What emotions come to mind? What do you value about it?

Professor of world missiology Roger Greenway writes, "It may be helpful to those who harbor misgivings about cities...to reflect on the fact that urbanization as a present fact of life for most of the human family is a reality under the providential control of God... By means of these enormous gatherings of people, God provides the church with one of history's greatest opportunities for evangelization. Pressed together in metropolises, the races, the tribes, and diverse groups are geographically more accessible than ever before... God in our time is moving climactically through a variety of social, political, and economic factors to bring earth's peoples into closer contact with one another, into greater interaction and interdependence, and into earshot of the gospel. By this movement God carries forward his redemptive purposes in history. A sign of our time is the city. Through worldwide migration to the city God may be setting the stage for Christian mission's greatest and perhaps final hour."[4]

[3] J.N. Manokaran, *Christ and Cities: Transformation of Urban Centres* (India: Mission Educational Books, 2005), 13.
[4] Roger Greenway, "World Urbanization and Missiological Education", in *Missiological Education for the 21st Century* (New York: Orbis, 1996), 145–146.

3. We heard in the DVD that,

> In the city you are going to find people that appear spiritually hopeless. You're going to find people of no religion, people of other religions, and people with deeply non-Christian lifestyles, and you're going to discover that many of them are kinder, deeper, and wiser than you. You will also find that many of the poor and the broken are much more open to the gospel of grace and more dedicated to its practical out-working than you are.

Has this been the case in your own experience or in the experience of people you know? Share examples.

Discuss with your group.

4. It is often said that Christians today have little impact on the world around them. Is that a correct assessment? Why? What prevents us from becoming more engaged in the world around us?

God calls us to be deeply engaged in the world so we may serve the world—yet we must not lose our own distinctive spiritual identity. As the culture becomes more secular, the task of being "in but not of" the world becomes complex and difficult.

Consider the following:

- It is far easier not to publicly proclaim the gospel, and particularly to avoid preaching the tougher parts about sin, hell, and repentance. A lack of preaching the complete gospel is no gospel at all, and therefore has no power to transform lives.

- It is difficult to engage and attract secular people. Doing so requires thought, time, and effort.

- It is far simpler to either reflect the surrounding culture or to disdain it. It is hard to avoid simple cultural confrontation or cultural assimilation and instead become agents for cultural renewal and enrichment.

- It is sometimes hard not to be judgmental and exclusive toward those who differ from us. Others can sense this in us.

Christianity is not simply a set of beliefs to be held in order to save my individual soul. It is also an interpretation of—and a distinct way of understanding—everything in the world. Both ancient Greek and modern thought, however, tend to separate faith and beliefs from the rest of life in what is known as "dualism." Dualism seals off personal beliefs and faith from the way we actually live and work in the world.

Moreover, it leads to a widespread assumption that the only way to truly serve God is through direct ministry—teaching, evangelizing, discipling. The church and its activities are seen as good and untainted, while the secular world is bad and polluting. This feeling is understandable. Many workplaces are so filled with excessive competition, superficiality, politics, greed, and cruelty that it is tempting to leave a secular job and just minister within the context of Christian community. Even if we don't do that, we may still simply opt to spend our life in more traditional, less difficult environments. This has effectively removed Christians from places of cultural influence.

The Bible does not support a sacred versus secular distinction. We cannot separate our faith from our work and our life in the public sphere. Every part of our lives—work, family, civic involvement, recreation—is to be done for God's glory. The Bible tells us that Jesus has to be Lord of every area of life, not just of our private lives. The gospel shapes and affects the motives, manner, and methods with which we carry out every task in life. Living like this is not easy, but it offers a profound way to have an impact on the world around us.

5. The Hebrew word translated "prosper" means "to be healthy, to increase, to have things go well." It means growth in all its dimensions. What types of growth within the Christian community can prosper the places in which we live?

We are to grow into the character of Christ. "But the fruit of the Spirit is love, joy, peace, patience, kindness, goodness, faithfulness, gentleness and self-control... Those who belong to Christ Jesus have crucified the sinful nature with its passions and desires" (Gal. 5:22–24). We are also to "grow in the grace and knowledge of our Lord and Savior Jesus Christ" (2 Peter 3:18) and "overflow with hope by the power of the Holy Spirit" (Rom. 15:13).

A church should also grow in the maturity of its fellowship and relationships within the body. Through Christ "the whole body...builds itself up in love, as each part does its work" (Eph. 4:16).

As we grow in these ways, we will also grow in Christ's passion for the lost. And so we will reach out in love to those who don't believe.

As we grow in these ways, we, as a community, will be better able and willing to discern the needs occurring in our neighborhoods and the gifts Christ has given us for meeting them. We will have a vision for what our neighborhoods should look like, not just a vision for our church. We will show in our words and our deeds that we want to promote the welfare of our neighborhoods in every way.

Also, we will live out our lives in love and service to others. We will seek to help the poor, the broken, and the marginalized and work for social justice.

6. In what specific ways can you and your group seek to serve and love your place of residence, rather than resemble it, or remove yourselves from it? What can you and your group do to become genuinely interested in its peace and prosperity?

To quote the DVD, "If we are to seek the peace and prosperity of our cities (and by city I mean any place of density and diversity and cultural energy) then we need to think about how to restore the city's original purposes. So, firstly, we serve and love those who need help and protection. We seek to serve the needs of others, no matter what their race or class, instead of seeking to use others to meet our own needs. Second, we need to "do justice"—we need to bring God's love, peace, and justice to bear on a broken world. Third, we create and cultivate culture with all that involves in terms of creativity and relationships and excellence and how we live out our faith in the workplace. And, fourth, we need to be a people who encourage others to seek spiritually—but hold out Christ as the ultimate satisfaction of that quest."

If the Jews—brought to Babylon in chains by a violent oppressor nation—were to see themselves as "carried" by God to seek the city's peace and prosperity (Jer. 29:7), then surely we are! We must see that God has specific ministry purposes for us in the place in which we live.

Examples include:

- Becoming involved in a ministry that helps people in need.

- Beginning a specific and consistent prayer ministry. Praying for specific neighborhoods, for particular people groups, and for specific problems. Using local newspapers to find things to pray for.

- Becoming more conscious of how the gospel can shape the way we work.

- Considering how to share our faith with colleagues and neighbors more boldly, persistently, lovingly, and joyfully.

[*Remember that at the end of this study you will need to briefly describe the purpose of the* Home Studies *to your group. Be enthusiastic about these studies—if you are eager to complete them, your group will be too.*]

[*Pray for your group.*]

Notes for Leaders

Session 2 Heart Three Ways To Live

[*Complete the* Home Study *on pages 14–30.*]

Bible Study Notes For Leaders

[*Read Luke 18:9–14 and then work through the questions and notes below ahead of time to help you prepare to lead your group. The notes beneath the questions are not intended as answers to be read aloud. They are notes to help you facilitate the discussion.*]

1. Look at what the Pharisee says about himself in verses 11 and 12. Is the Pharisee a hypocrite? Discuss.

There were certainly people who said they were righteous, but were murdering people. There's no indication of that here. This is a good man. When he says he gives a tenth of all he gets, that means he's generous to the poor. When he says he doesn't commit adultery, that means he's a faithful husband.

When we look at the prayer, though, we see that what Jesus gives us is almost a caricature. Whenever you write a thank-you letter to somebody, aren't you thanking them for things that they have done? Whenever you start a prayer like this, "I thank you, Lord, that," what do you expect? When you say, "I thank you, Lord," afterward there's supposed to be a reference to the things that God has done.

But the Pharisee says, "God, I thank you," and that's it. That's the last reference to God. The prayer is all about the Pharisee himself. This is self-worship. Underneath the veneer of God-centeredness is utter self-centeredness. Underneath the veneer of all the God-talk and all the God-activity and all the morality is adoration of self.

2. What does the Pharisee understand righteousness to be and how to achieve it?

His approach to righteousness has two marks:

Externalism

The Pharisee's understanding of sin and virtue is completely external. It's completely focused on behavior and the violation of, or keeping of, rules. It's not looking inside; it's not looking at character. Sin is perceived completely in terms of discrete, individual actions.

He says, "I do not rob. I do not commit adultery. I do not cheat. I give my money away. I fast. I do my religious observances." Notice he doesn't say, "God, I thank you that I'm getting more patient. I'm getting to be a gentler person. I'm able to love people I used to not be able to love. I'm able to keep my joy and my peace, even when things go wrong." He's not talking about those things. He is absolutely externally focused.

His understanding of sin and of virtue is completely oriented to external behavior—keeping and breaking rules.

Comparison

He says, "I'm not like other men," implying, "I am so much better." Verse 9 says he's looking down on "everybody else."

Notice something very interesting. The Pharisee thinks he is better than others because, "I am not a robber, evildoer or adulterer." Now, that's in the Bible—not stealing or doing evil or committing adultery. "Also I tithe." That's in the Bible.

And then he says, "I fast twice a week" (v. 12). There's nothing in the Bible about fasting twice a week. There's nothing in God's law that requires that. This is something he chose to do. He is taking a personal preference or a cultural custom, and he's elevating it and giving it moral significance, using it as a way of feeling more virtuous than other people.

3. The tax collector does not actually say what you see in the English translation of verse 13, "God, have mercy on me, *a* sinner." He uses a definite article in the Greek. He says, "God, have mercy on me, *the* sinner." What can we learn about repentance from the attitude of the tax collector?

If you think of sin externally and comparatively, like the Pharisee, there's always somebody who has committed more sins than you. You're only ever *a* sinner, you're never *the* sinner. This man, however, is thinking of sin in absolute terms. What he's saying is, "All I know is I'm lost, and where everybody else is doesn't matter."

The tax collector is not just looking at what he's done wrong; he's not just looking at his discrete individual actions, his whole understanding of himself is that he is *the sinner*—it is how he sees himself. It is a part of his identity. Ask the group to take time to make this personal. Is this a part of your and their identity?

He asks for "mercy." He sees his dependence on God's radical grace. Again, make this personal—i.e., ask the group to come up with personal examples and to apply this to their own life.

In *The Doctrine of Repentance*, the seventeenth-century preacher and author Thomas Watson gives six characteristics of real repentance.[1] They are based closely on Psalm 51. It may be helpful to review them with your group.

1. Sight of sin

"My sin is always before me." (v. 3)

You cannot really repent without the Holy Spirit giving you some illumination—making sin real to you.

2. Sorrow for sin

"Against you, you only, have I sinned and done what is evil in your sight." (v. 4a)

Real repentance involves real sorrow over sin and the way it has grieved God. False repentance is sorrow over the consequences of sin and the way it has grieved you. Self-pity may appear to be repentance, but it is not.

---

[1] Thomas Watson, *The Doctrine of Repentance* (Carlisle, Penn.: Banner of Truth, 1668), 18.

3. Confession of sin

"You are proved right when you speak and justified when you judge." (v. 4b)

Real repentance makes no excuses, shifts no blame, and takes full responsibility.

4. Shame for sin

"Surely I was sinful at birth." (v. 5)

In real repentance there is a change in your whole attitude toward yourself. You see yourself, like the tax collector, as "the sinner."

5. Hatred for sin

"What is evil in your sight." (v. 4)

If there has been real sorrow for the sin (and not just the consequences), then you will come to hate the sin in itself.

6. Turning from sin

"Grant me a willing spirit." (v. 12)

If the other five elements are there, somewhat in this order, you will forsake the sin. Its power over you will be weakened, and you will at least make progress out of it.

4. Pastor and author John Stott writes,

> 'Justification' is a legal term, borrowed from the law courts. It is the exact opposite of 'condemnation'. 'To condemn' is to declare somebody guilty; 'to justify' is to declare him...righteous. In the Bible it refers to God's act of unmerited favor by which He puts a sinner right with Himself, not only pardoning or acquitting him, but accepting him and treating him as righteous.[2]

Jesus says the tax collector went home "justified" before God. Why? What does this passage teach us about justification?

In the parable, Jesus introduces us to a universal problem, the problem of righteousness, and then gives us two figures, each of whom represents a particular solution to the problem. One solution does not work; one does.

 [2] John Stott, *The Message of Galatians* (Chicago, Ill.: IVP, 1968), 60.

You have the "good" man, the Pharisee; and you have a "bad" man, the tax collector. Tax collectors were collaborators, gangsters, shakedown artists. Yet, after they pray, Jesus concludes the "bad" man is the one who is justified before God.

Jesus is showing us something at the heart of the gospel. The Pharisee is trying to justify himself by his good deeds, by his religion. He is keeping God's rules, but in such a way—focusing on the external—that it makes him feel good about himself and he can say, "Now, God, you owe me." He is keeping God's rules as a way of earning his justification—he is not depending on God's radical grace.

The tax collector on the other hand shows by his words and actions (verse 13 says, "he would not even look up to heaven") that he is utterly depending on God's mercy.

We are justified, we are, as the quote says, treated as righteous, because of God's unmerited favor. God's love and acceptance of us is secured in Christ, and we obey God's law out of a desire to delight, resemble, and know him.

However, we often behave as if God's love and acceptance of us is based on the quality of our behavior and the purity of our hearts. We obey God's law out of a fear of rejection and out of a desire to create a good self-image through our moral efforts.

Some of the common ways we do this:

- If we cannot feel forgiven after a sin or failure until we have spent a great deal of time in misery and pain, we may be basing our acceptance with God on how much we have groveled, beaten ourselves up, and made ourselves miserable.

- If we are proud and harsh toward others, we may be basing our acceptance with God on moral standards that we believe we are fulfilling.

- If we feel like failures, filled with low self-esteem, we may be basing our acceptance with God on moral standards that we believe we are not fulfilling.

Read Luke 15:11–32 and watch the DVD for Session 2 to help you prepare to lead your group through the discussion that follows.

Discussion Questions Notes For Leaders

After watching the DVD with your group, use these questions to encourage discussion. The notes beneath the questions are not intended as answers to be read aloud. They are notes to help you facilitate the discussion.

You do not need to complete all the questions. Depending on the dynamic of the group and your time limit, you may find it helpful to choose in advance the questions that will be of most value to your group and start with those.

1. Was there anything from the DVD that was new to you, or had an effect on you? Did you hear anything that raised more questions in your mind?

Discuss with your group.

2. Which of the two brothers is easiest for you to identify with, and why?

Discuss with your group.

3. What emotions and attitudes does the elder brother display, and what does this show about his relationship with God?

"became angry" (v. 28)

He is filled with anger. One of the signs of a moralistic spirit is a feeling that God owes us a comfortable and good life if we live up to standards. This will lead to anger when life takes a bad turn. The anger can have one of two forms. If people feel they have been living right, they will be angry at God; if they feel that they have not been living right, they will be angry at themselves.

"I've been slaving for you" (v. 29)

He is full of joyless, mechanical obedience. Elder brothers don't do good out of delight in goodness itself, or for the pleasure of God. They do it, therefore, joylessly, slavishly. Christians are filled with amazement at the grace of God, and so obey out of delight in pleasing God for his own sake. This is not how the elder brother relates to God—he feels like a slave.

"you never threw me a party" (v. 29 paraphrase)

He lacks assurance of the father's love. There is no dancing or festiveness about the elder brother's relationship with his father. As long as people are trying to earn their salvation by controlling God through their goodness, they will never be sure they have "made it." There will always be anxiety and fear and uncertainty in the relationship.

"this son of yours" (v. 30)

He is cold to younger brother-types. The older son will not even "own" his brother. He has no love for or longing to see his brother—unlike the father in the story. Elder brothers are disdainful of or ineffective in evangelism, whereas the person changed by the gospel is always disposed toward evangelism. First, if people believe they are sinners saved by grace alone, they will not feel superior to anyone else—not to other cultural or racial groups, not to other faiths, not to immoral people. Second, if people understand the gospel, they will treat others with hope. They will never look at anyone and say, "Here's someone who could never become a Christian," because they know that all "types" of people are equally unlikely to find God.

"who has squandered your property with prostitutes" (v. 30)

He has an unforgiving, judgmental spirit. He highlights the fact that the younger brother has been with "prostitutes," while he has been living a chaste life at home. Elder brothers lack two things necessary to forgive. On the one hand, they lack the emotional humility to say, "I'm no different." Instead they look at the sinner and say, "I would never do that!" On the other hand, they lack the emotional "wealth" to say, "I am so loved and forgiven by my father—what does it matter that I was slighted or wronged?" He cannot forgive the younger brother, unlike the father, who is so lavish in his forgiveness.

4. What do you think it means "to repent not only of our bad things, but also for the reason we did our good things"?

What makes someone a Christian is not simply repenting of sin. Of course Christians must repent of their sins, but remember that the Pharisees also repent of their sins. When they break one of God's laws they repent—they repent often—but it doesn't make them Christians, only elder brothers.

Christians not only repent of what they've done that's bad, but they also repent of the very reason they've done good—their desire (like the elder brother's) to be their own savior and put God in their debt and therefore under control.

This means that we need to recognize that the reasons for our righteous deeds have been the same as the reasons for our sins—to seek to control our own lives and even God; to be our own savior and lord. The moment we begin to repent of that sin is the moment our whole life changes. It is called "new birth," because it is a radical, utter transformation. It means a change of our foundational trusts and hopes. It means a change in our very identity—what gives us our basic value and distinctiveness. Born again!

People will never "find their way home" if they just repent of sins and try to live a better life. That does not bring fundamental heart change. It does not disturb the basic orientation of self-salvation that is the problem in both the lives of the "good" people and the "bad" people. We must not just repent for being bad, but also for the underlying reason we've been good.

5. **"If I gave you a test on justification by grace alone through faith alone through the substitutionary work of Christ alone, you'd probably get 100 percent." If we're justified by grace alone, not by our good works or our moral efforts or anything we can do, what motivates us to live an obedient, repentant life?**

If you know that there is "no condemnation for those who are in Christ Jesus" (Rom. 8:1), there is all the motivation in the world to live an obedient, repentant life. Here are just some aspects of it:

We live an obedient, repentant life because we want to delight the Lord who saved us

Our continual experience of the grace and love of God in the gospel grows within us a desire to bring God delight and pleasure.

We live an obedient, repentant life because we want to honor and resemble the Lord

There is a deep human instinct to imitate what we admire and honor. To honor great people, for example, we make images of them—statues and paintings—and we urge people to emulate them. A godly life is the deepest way to honor the one who lived and died to serve and save us. We want to be images of him.

We live an obedient, repentant life because we want to have fellowship with God

We want to sense God's presence, and living life for him is the way to do that.

6. If Jesus is our true elder brother, how does it change the way we live on a daily basis?

The following are only some of the wonderful and innumerable implications of the fact that Jesus Christ is our true elder brother:

- He should be the ultimate beauty and satisfaction for our hearts. He is not simply to be admired and respected, but worshiped, adored, and delighted in. The purpose of our lives is to behold his glory (John 17:24), and that certainly means more than simply believing in him or even obeying him. He is the ultimate object of worship. He is to be reveled in, savored, and rejoiced in.

- He is to be absolutely obeyed and given the central priority of our lives. He should be the preeminent concern of our choices, the ultimate Lord over our wills. We need to be reading the Bible to learn better how to do this.

- He should bring complete rest and assurance to our consciences. His salvation is of infinite value. His blood was shed as a ransom (Mark 10:45) to pay for our sins. This blood was the blood of God (Acts 20:28). Imagine how valuable that is. No sin is too great to be forgiven; no corruption is too great to be healed.

- We should not be impressed with glitz, physical beauty, status, and power. The incarnation means that God was willing to empty himself of his glory and power and live humbly as a servant. He associated with "undesirables." We should not rely on appearances or prefer the more privileged and elite circles. The incarnation should mean the end of our snobbery.

- We live with infallible hope. Jesus, the true King, has begun to put the world right with his power. Right now that healing is only partial, but some day all deformity, decay, sin, disease, and imperfection will be wiped away.

[*Pray for your group.*]

Notes for Leaders

Session 3 Idolatry The Sin Beneath The Sin

[*Complete the* Home Study *on pages 36–50.*]

[*Complete the* Home Study *on pages 36–50.*]

Bible Study Notes For Leaders

[*Read Romans 1:18–25 and then work through the questions and notes below ahead of time to help you prepare to lead your group. The notes beneath the questions are not intended as answers to be read aloud. They are notes to help you facilitate the discussion.*]

1. What is the reason that our minds and hearts become "futile" and "darkened"? (Look especially at verse 21a.)

In verse 21, Paul tells us the basic reason is that even though deep down we know we owe God everything, we want to control our lives—so we create idols.

We do not "glorify" God. That is, we do not act toward him as if he really were as great, supreme, and central as he actually is.

We do not "thank" God. That is, we fail to act toward him as if we really were as totally dependent and indebted to him as we actually are. A lack of appropriate gratitude reveals a heart that does not want to admit its own limitations. It wants to think of itself as far more self-sufficient than it really is.

We "suppress" (v. 18) these facts because we don't want to admit our complete allegiance to God. We want to be our own masters.

2. According to these verses, what are some of the results of idolatry in our lives? Has this been true in your own experience? Share examples.

In verse 25, Paul tells us that rejecting God's control of our lives leads inevitably to constructing counterfeit gods or idols. We cannot simply deny the glory of God (v. 21); we must "exchange the glory of God" for the glory of something else (v. 23). We must glorify something—we must worship, adore, and build our lives on something as an ultimate value. Since we were created for worship, we cannot eliminate God without creating God-substitutes or idols.

Because God created the world, all created things have some of God's glory in them, so it is appropriate to find these things great, wonderful, and admirable. The problem comes from giving any created thing inordinate affection—affection that is ultimate, like that which we owe God. If we do this:

We are deceived

"They exchanged the truth of God for a lie" (v. 25). Compare this with verse 21 where it says that as a result of rejecting God, "their thinking became futile and their foolish hearts were darkened."

At the base of every one of our life choices, our emotional structures, and our personalities is a false belief system centered on an idol, something besides God that we think can give us the significance and joy that only God can give. We look to something besides Jesus to be our "savior," our "righteousness."

Of course, nothing and no one but God can possibly hold this kind of power. Idols can never satisfy, but we live in denial of this. So every idol leads us to create a delusion, spinning out a whole set of false definitions of success, happiness, and worth. Our hearts operate out of deep false beliefs, such as, "If I can just achieve _____, then I will be happy," or "Because I lost _____, I can never be happy."

Paul shows how comprehensive this delusion, blindness, and deception can be. It consists of intellectual confusion and frustration (v. 21, "their thinking became futile"), and of emotional confusion and frustration (v. 21, "hearts were darkened ").

Even so, we will never blame the idol itself. We will blame God, the world, our own failures, or the failure of others.

We are enslaved

"God gave them over in the sinful desires of their hearts" (v. 24). This tells us that our heart's desires, growing inordinate and uncontrollable through idolatry, simply sweep us away. We are given over to them.

In verse 25, Paul says that we not only worship our idols, but we serve or obey them. Human beings are goal-oriented. To live in the world, we order our lives into priorities. Whatever becomes the bottom line—that which defines and validates all other things—we will feel absolutely driven to do. We are given over to it. It controls us. We have to have it in order to be happy, to like ourselves, to have meaning in life. And since this substitute does not satisfy, because our hearts were made to center on God, rather than on any created thing, we always need more and more. We are given over to our idols.

3. What do these verses tell us about the wrath of God?

Its existence

Some may question how this can be, or say, "I have trouble with this." In this situation, a guiding question can be: "If you deeply love a person, does that preclude wrath?"

Its presence

It is here now. Note the present tense "is being revealed."

Its object

It is against "godlessness" (a word which refers to disregard of God's rights) and "wickedness" (which, strictly speaking, refers to disregard of human rights to love, truth, justice, etc.).

Its deservedness

It is against people who know better, who "suppress the truth." This important idea of "suppressing the truth" shows that every person "down deep" knows there is a God to whom they owe allegiance. Verse 21 goes so far as to say all human beings, even the pagans "knew God." (This doesn't mean that they had a personal covenant relationship with him, but that their knowledge of God's existence is very real, though repressed.)

It's the reason we need the gospel

The NIV translation leaves out the word "for" which (in the Greek) starts verse 18. The word connects verse 18 with verses 16–17 and shows us that the gospel is necessary because there is such a thing as the wrath of God.

All of Paul's confidence, joy, and passion for the gospel (Rom. 1:1–17) rests upon the assumption that all human beings are, apart from the gospel, under the wrath of God. If you don't understand or believe in the wrath of God, the gospel will not thrill, empower, or move you.

The justice of God's wrath can only be understood by looking at the self-destructive power of evil. Darkened hearts and minds are the direct results of a refusal of the truth (note the connection of vv. 21a and 21b). The bondage they experience emotionally is the result of worshiping false gods that cannot satisfy (note the connection of vv. 23 and 24). In other words, sin is violating the order God created (e.g., God created us to serve him; God created us to live unselfish lives; God created us to tell the truth).

God's wrath and punishment is to "give us over" (v. 24a) to the things we worship and the things we want. We see both the justice yet terror of God's wrath. It is just, because "down deep" we know that there is a God (v. 20, "without excuse") and he is only giving us what we want. It is terrible, because it means that the worst thing God can do to a human being is to let them reach their idolatrous goals.

Note: Don't let this discussion go on for too long.

4. John Calvin describes us as "a perpetual factory of idols."[1] What are some examples of personal idols?

Any thing can become an idol, including good things. Examples of personal idols:

Work and career

Work becomes the most important thing to you—to be productive and useful, or to feel successful and powerful.

Notes for Leaders

Beauty and image

This can show itself in various forms, including the following:

- You are prone to eating disorders and to spending excessive time, effort, and concern on appearance.

- You need the "false intimacy" of pornography and other anonymous sex.

Family

This idolatry has many variations:

- Your children's prospects, happiness, obedience, health, or godliness become the most important thing.

- Meeting your parents' expectations becomes the most important thing.

- Getting married or having a "perfect" marriage becomes the most important thing.

Romance

This is not the same as pure sexual gratification. You live for "falling in love," or for someone to love you, or for the dream of some true love that will fix everything.

Money

This idolatry has many variations:

- Having (and saving) lots of money may be your security, the main way you feel safe in the world.

- Having (and spending) lots of money may be your main way of feeling significant and important.

You may want to tie this study back to the previous session by mentioning that the younger and elder brothers in the parable in Luke 15 represent some very common idols. You may want to use the table on page 43 to help the group identify those idols.

[*Watch the DVD for Session 3 to help you prepare to lead your group through the discussion that follows.*]

¹ John Calvin, *Institutes of the Christian Religion*, Battles Edition, Book 1, Chapter XI, Section 8 (Philadelphia: Westminster Press, 1960), 108.

Discussion Questions Notes For Leaders

After watching the DVD with your group, use these questions to encourage discussion. The notes beneath the questions are not intended as answers to be read aloud. They are notes to help you facilitate the discussion.

You do not need to complete all the questions. Depending on the dynamic of the group and your time limit, you may find it helpful to choose in advance the questions that will be of most value to your group and start with those.

1. Was there anything from the DVD that was new to you, or had an effect on you? Did you hear anything that raised more questions in your mind?

Discuss with your group.

2. "If you really want to change…Jesus Christ must become your over-mastering positive passion." When and how have you found this to be true in your experience or in the lives of people you know?

Below are some examples of ways to remember and pray that Christ is your over-mastering positive passion when certain emotions crop up because some idol has gained ascendency:

When you feel anxiety

Rejoice and pray, "All the things I have are gifts of grace because of Christ's love and sacrifice. They aren't here because of my performance, but because of his generosity. Christ loved me enough to sacrifice himself for me; he will continue to give me what I need. Be consoled, Self."

When you feel pride and anger

Rejoice and pray, "All the things I have are gifts of grace because of Christ's love and sacrifice. I have never received what I deserve—and I never will. If God gave me what I deserved, I'd be dead. Be humbled, Self."

When you feel guilt

Rejoice and pray, "All the things I have are gifts of grace because of Christ's love and sacrifice. I never earned them to begin with, so I can't un-earn them. Christ loved and loves me, even though he knew I would do this. Be confident, Self."

When you feel boredom and lethargy

Rejoice and pray, "All the things I have are gifts of grace because of Christ's love and sacrifice. The very fact I am a Christian is a miracle. Be amazed. Be in wonder, Self."

3. Archbishop William Temple said, "Your religion is what you do with your solitude."[2] When you are alone what do you tend to think about most? Where do your thoughts go naturally, instinctively, habitually? How does this help identify your idols?

Temple's quote leads us to imagine ourselves standing on a corner, waiting for someone for a long time. We have nothing to read, to listen to, to look at, or to do. Here is the question: When your mind is completely unfettered and able to dwell wherever it wishes, what do you think about most naturally, instinctively, and habitually?

Do your thoughts go to God—to his excellence, his attributes, his glory, his beauty? Is that where your mind and heart go automatically? Wherever they go (Temple indicates), there you find your real god, your ultimate concern, the thing your heart most rests in and worships.

We should love God so much that he dominates our solitude. We should love God so much that we are content in any circumstance, because we always have what we most want in life. Of course, this is never true of us. Other things usurp God's place, and what we do with our solitude is one of the indicators of what those things, those idols, are.

---

[2] This quote is attributed to Sir William Temple, English diplomat, statesman, essayist and author (1628–1699).

4. "Under every behavioral sin is the sin of idolatry, and under every act of idolatry is a disbelief in the gospel." Do you agree? Why or why not? What are the implications for how we really change our hearts and lives?

Luther saw that the Old Testament law against idols and the New Testament emphasis on justification by faith alone are essentially the same.[3] He says that failure to believe that God accepts us fully in Christ—and looking to something else for our salvation—is a failure to keep the first commandment, namely, having no other gods before him. Why? If you try to earn your own salvation through works-righteousness, then you must be, by definition, looking to something else to be your savior, even if that "something else" is your own moral record and performance.

The Ten Commandments begin with two commands against idolatry, followed by the other eight. Why this order? It is because the fundamental problem in law-breaking is idolatry.

- In other words, we never break commandments three through to ten without first breaking commandments one and two.
- We would not lie, commit adultery, kill, etc. unless we were first making some other thing, or things, more of an ultimate hope and value to us than God.
  - We would not steal if God were our real wealth.
  - We would not commit adultery if God were our real beauty.
  - We would not lie unless there were something we needed to have—honor or power or approval or control—more than God.
- Though we may intellectually accept the gospel of salvation by grace alone through Christ alone, at the moment we sin our hearts are looking to something else as our hope and salvation.

Thus, beneath any particular sin is this sin of rejecting Christ-salvation and indulging in self-salvation.

[3] See Martin Luther, *A Treatise on Good Works* (Whitefish, Mont.: Kessinger, n.d.).

In Colossians, Paul says, "Put to death, therefore, whatever belongs to your earthly nature: sexual immorality, impurity, lust, evil desires [*epithumiai*] and greed, which is idolatry" (Col. 3:5). The term "evil desires" is the Greek word *epithumiai*. The word means an "*epi*-desire"—a mega or inordinate desire—so Paul is saying, "Kill off your hearts' over-desires, which are caused by idolatry." We break the first commandment every day when we put more of our hearts' trust for our significance and security in created things rather than in Jesus. This creates inordinate longings and emotional attachment to these things, even if they are good in themselves.

Paul goes on to say, "Set your minds on things above...your life is now hidden with Christ in God. When Christ, who is your life, appears, then you also will appear with him in glory" (Col. 3:2–4). Here we get a strategy to use on our own hearts. When you are wracked by epi-anger, fear, despondency, or some other inordinate emotion, recognize the idol beneath it and say, "You are not my life. You do not define me. Christ is my life. You did not die for me, and you cannot redeem me. He did and can and will! So ultimately, I don't really have to have you." When Paul says we must "set our minds" on Christ, he certainly is talking about more than just thinking. He means we are to come into Christ's presence in prayer and rely on the Holy Spirit to make him spiritually real to our hearts.

The only way we can really fundamentally change, then, is not simply through moral reformation but through ever deeper repentance for our idols, and ever deeper faith and joy in Jesus Christ as our Savior and Lord.

Only when Jesus, through the gospel, becomes the greatest object of our affection—because he is the source of our salvation, joy, hope, meaning, and worth—will we change. No one can change simply through "willpower." We will always be controlled by our heart's supreme affection and love, by our heart's ultimate source of love and meaning, by our idols. There is no other way to truly change one's heart and character than through the grace of the gospel.

5. In his book *Gods That Fail*, Vinoth Ramachandra quotes Psalm 115 on idols: "Those who make them will be like them, and so will all who trust in them." He writes, "Note the shattering conclusion: we become like what we worship."[4] Do we? In what way and why?

Ramachandra continues, "The logic of this psalm follows from the biblical doctrine of humanness. We are created in the image of the God whose true likeness is disclosed to us in the human figure of Jesus Christ. Worship involves a restoration of our 'fallen' humanity to this true definition of what it means to be human. We may not notice this transformation into Christ-like humanness, but others will. Likewise, when we worship that in whose image we were *not* created it *will* show in our lives."[5]

In his book *We Become What We Worship*, G.K. Beale writes, "God has made all people to reflect, to be imaging beings. People will always reflect something, whether it be God's character or some feature of the world. If people are committed to God, they will become like him; if they are committed to something other than God, they will become like that thing, always spiritually inanimate and empty like the lifeless and vain aspect of creation to which they have committed themselves... We become spiritually blind, deaf and dumb even though we have physical eyes and ears. If we commit ourselves to something that does not have God's Spirit, to that degree we will be lacking the Spirit... The point is that our lives become vain and empty when we commit ourselves to vain idols of this world."[6]

6. What are some of the concrete ways we can make Christ King and Lord of our entire lives?

To treat Jesus as King and Lord means:

Obeying

That is, to comply with God's commands in his Word unconditionally.

- An example of failing to obey unconditionally is Jonah. He could not see how preaching to Nineveh would help him or his nation.
- If Jesus is Lord, however, you must obey even if you don't understand why.
- The evaluation question to ask is, "Am I willing to obey whatever God says about this area of my life, no matter how I feel about it?"

[4] Vinoth Ramachandra, *Gods That Fail* (Downers Grove, Ill.: IVP, 1996), 115. [5] Ibid.

Submitting

That is, to accept trials or suffering as part of God's plan.

- An example of failing to submit is Job. He thought God was unfair, that nothing good could come out of his suffering.

- If Jesus is Lord, however, you must submit to him in the things he sends your way.

- The evaluation question to ask is, "Am I willing to thank God for whatever happens in this area, whether I understand it or not?" (This is not the same as believing that God is happy to send tragedy. Rather, it is believing that God, in his overall purpose for your life, is always acting wisely and redemptively.)

Relying

That is, that Jesus should hold the title to your heart's deepest allegiance, loyalty, trust, and love.

- An example of failing to rely on God is Abraham. His temptation was to make Isaac an idol. Isaac could become what Abraham relied on more than God for his joy and meaning in life.

- If Jesus is Lord, however, you will rely on him and nothing else.

- The evaluation question is, "Is there something in this area I am relying on more than God for my hope and meaning in life?"

Expecting

That is, that you should expect God to use his power and resources on your behalf.

- An example of failing to expect great things is Moses. When he was called, his sense of incompetence prevented him from immediately embracing God's charge.

- If Jesus is Lord, however, you need to expect that he would not call you to do something without supporting you.

- The evaluation question is, "Are there problems or limitations in my life that I think are too big for God to remove?"

[*Pray for your group.*]

6 G.K. Beale, *We Become What We Worship: A Biblical Theology of Idolatry* (Downers Grove, Ill.: IVP, 2008), 302–308.

Notes for Leaders

Session 4 Community The Context For Change

[*Complete the* Home Study *on pages 56–72.*]

Bible Study Notes For Leaders

[*Read Philippians 2:1–11 and then work through the questions and notes below ahead of time to help you prepare to lead your group. The notes beneath the questions are not intended as answers to be read aloud. They are notes to help you facilitate the discussion.*]

1. Looking at verses 2–4, what can we infer is the problem that Paul is addressing in the Philippian church?

We can imagine what the problems are by looking at the positive exhortations. First, in verse 2, he asks them to be "like-minded, having the same love, being one in spirit and purpose." This is a call to unity, but it is a threefold call, to mind, heart, and will. He wants them to agree on the truth ("like-minded"), love one another ("having the same love"), and work together toward the same goal ("being one in spirit and purpose").

Verses 3 through 4 are a call to humility, to putting others' interests ahead of their own. While verse 2 addressed the Christians as an entire body, verses 3 and 4 address each one as an individual. They are to turn from two things: "selfish ambition" (which is putting their own needs ahead of others) and "vain conceit" (which is an unrealistic assessment of themselves).

It seems that self-centeredness was leading to disunity in this church.

2. What are the four grounds for unity and humility that Paul lists in verse 1? How do these grounds lead to unity and humility?

The "encouragement from being united with Christ"

The word "encouragement" is the Greek word *paraklesis*, which means to be "strengthened" and given courage from our salvation in Christ.

The "comfort" of Christ's love

The word "comfort" connotes the consolation you give someone who is grieving.

The Spirit's "fellowship"

The word means "participation."

"Tenderness and compassion"

These two words are used frequently in the Bible to describe God's mercy.

Paul is saying that they have strength and deep consolation from Christ. They have been bound together by the participation in one Spirit, and they have been freely forgiven by the mercy of the Father.

There are many ways these grounds lead to unity and humility. Here are just a few:

- The strength and deep consolation from Christ should make us less needy. The term "vain conceit" connotes being hungry for honor, recognition, and status. If we have profound joy, encouragement, and consolation from Christ, we should not need the approbation of others.

- The "participation of the Spirit" means that all Christians are one, despite their differences. We may have diverse opinions, temperaments, or cultural mind-sets—but the fact that we all participate in the Spirit should be more important than political, intellectual, or cultural differences.

- The remembrance of the mercy of God should first humble us and second be a model for us. God's care and provision for us was completely unmerited and undeserved, so we should humble ourselves before others.

3. Verse 5 says, "Your attitude should be the same as that of Christ Jesus." What do we learn about Jesus' attitude from verses 6–11?

The incarnation (vv. 6–7)

Here we see that Jesus, though he had a divine nature (v. 6a, "being in very nature God"), made himself nothing by "taking the very nature of a servant" (v. 7). Paul does not say that Jesus shed his nature as God, but rather he assumed a human nature. Jesus was, then, both divine and human at the same time.

The atonement (v. 8)

Jesus did not simply humble himself into being a man, but he also humbled himself to a particular task. He "became obedient to death—even death on a cross!" Despite the fact that he retained his divine nature when on the earth, he voluntarily did not exercise his rights, but instead became weak and vulnerable and died on the cross for us.

The future kingdom (vv. 9–11)

This section tells us that God exalted Jesus "to the highest place" (v. 9). He is exalted and ruling from heaven. Paul looks all the way forward to the day when everyone and everything in the world will bow the knee to Jesus.

Jesus' life was marked by not just one but two self-humblings: the incarnation and the cross. He *was* exalted—but by God, and only through and after his humbling.

Jesus turned away from personal glory and gain voluntarily, deliberately, and decisively. He shows us that the way to lead is to serve. The way to find fulfillment is not to seek fulfillment but look to the fulfillment of others.

4. In his book *Love in Hard Places* Don Carson writes,

> The church is...made up of natural enemies. What binds us together is not common education, common race, common income levels, common politics, common nationality, common accents, common jobs, or anything else of that sort. Christians come together...because they have all been saved by Jesus Christ and owe him a common allegiance... They are a band of natural enemies who love one another for Jesus' sake.[1]

Do you agree with his assessment? Why or why not? Share examples.

One of the most important ways that the Christian church embodies the gospel is in the unity of Christians who are different from one another—temperamentally, culturally, and racially. We need to show the world that people who cannot live in love and unity outside of Christ can do so in Christ.

When it comes to building actual relationships across racial and cultural barriers, we quickly come up against a host of attitudes, rooted deeply in our own cultural customs and ways of thinking, that make it hard to accept and respect people of other groups. We are "natural enemies." The gospel works to overcome these attitudes. We are sinners saved by sheer grace, and we need to draw out the implications and live in total consistency with that.

Read 1 Peter 2:9–12 and watch the DVD for Session 4 to help you prepare to lead your group through the discussion that follows.

[1] D. A. Carson, *Love In Hard Places* (Wheaton, Ill.: Crossway, 2002), 61.

Discussion Questions Notes For Leaders

After watching the DVD with your group, use these questions to encourage discussion. The notes beneath the questions are not intended as answers to be read aloud. They are notes to help you facilitate the discussion.

You do not need to complete all the questions. Depending on the dynamic of the group and your time limit, you may find it helpful to choose in advance the questions that will be of most value to your group and start with those.

1. Was there anything from the DVD that was new to you, or had an effect on you? Did you hear anything that raised more questions in your mind?

Discuss with your group.

2. We heard in the DVD that,

> We are "a holy nation"—different, distinct from the world and the people around us. And yet at the same time, we're supposed to be "a royal priesthood"—deeply involved in the lives of the world and the people around us.

Do you feel that you are part of the sort of community described in the DVD? If not, why not? What can you do to make this happen?

Discuss with your group.

3. "We will not know God, change deeply, nor win the world apart from community." To what extent have you experienced this?

Discuss with your group.

4. What practices make a good, strong, healthy Christian community? Brainstorm practical ways by which your own group can deepen its life together as a community.

The idea of community cannot be squared with merely attending church on Sunday—even regularly. The biblical texts imply a far deeper involvement. Our community needs to be marked by:

Cross-cultural unity

- When we believe the gospel, we receive a profound union with others who believe, even though they may be radically different from us in every other way. We should be making close friends with people from groupings, classes, or races who, apart from the gospel, we'd never know or care to know.

- It is worth noting that the unity of the church is a deeply missional factor (John 17:23). The early churches of the Mediterranean world were multi-ethnic, consisting of at least Jews and Greeks but often Africans and Asians too (see Acts 13:1 and following). Peter speaks of them collectively as "a chosen people, a royal priesthood, a holy nation, a people belonging to God" (1 Peter 2:9).

Counter-cultural distinctiveness

- When Peter calls us a "holy nation," he is saying, literally, that we are a distinct, unique community—a group of people who have distinct ways of doing nearly everything. We are a counter-culture in which we help each other become distinctive in everything we do:
    - how we use money and possessions
    - how we conduct relationships and family life
    - how we do our work
    - how we love and serve the poor and marginalized, and so on.

Corporate spirituality

- We should be praying with others.
- We should experience God with other people with some consistency.

Personal accountability

- We should be accountable personally to some others. We should have shared enough of our lives with others so that they see whether we are growing in Christ and can support us.

As well as all the other factors you may mention, including those from Philippians that you considered earlier, make sure to note that the "one another" commands that were examined in detail in the *Home Study* (the nine community-building practices) on pages 58–72 also contribute to a good, strong, healthy Christian community. You may want to review these briefly together as a group.

Some practical ways by which your own group can deepen its life together as a community include:

Common time

- Community requires availability. You must not be too hard for others to reach.
- Community requires frequency. There must be plenty of time shared together regularly.

Common practices

- Community requires a variety of practices:
  - eating together
  - recreation and often attending church together
  - learning together (Bible study, reading, and reflection in general)
  - personal counsel, comfort, and specific accountability for behavior
  - commitment to constant reconciliation and forgiveness
  - deeds of service and justice and witness done together
  - prayer, worship, and making music together

Common resources

- Community requires sharing home and living space through hospitality with others.
- Community requires sharing our resources, and feeling a sense of responsibility to others.

- To be involved deeply in people's lives is hard spiritual work. C.S. Lewis said that the only way to be sure not to have your heart broken is to never give it to anyone.[2] As Christians, we will and must give our hearts to others. Love is not only an action, but must also be an inner attitude of good will, patience, forgiveness, and warmth toward others.

5. How can we love people we do not naturally like?

Can we do loving deeds even when we don't "feel" loving? As we carry out loving deeds in spite of how we feel, can we work on our hearts to put aside condescension, irritability, bias, and selfishness?

We must remember Jesus' sacrifice for us when we try to "love people we do not naturally like." How does this work?

- The gospel is this: we are not loved because we are lovely, but in spite of our unloveliness. We are not loved because we have made ourselves worthy of love, but because Jesus died for us when we were unattractive in order to make us attractive.

- If Christians think of this as they are serving unattractive people, they will find a growing degree of repentance. "Loving Father, I was so much more unattractive to you than this person is to me, yet you were tortured and killed—you gave up your life for me! And all I need to do is to give up some time and effort for this person."

- A person who does not understand the gospel cannot do this. People who are just generally moral and nice cannot do this. They have to choose between the two inadequate alternatives, either phony love (niceness toward people you dislike) or sporadic love (kindness only toward people you like).

- If you show love as you repent, however, your heart is softened as you serve. Your service is sincere toward God at that moment and becomes more sincere toward people as you go along.

---

[2] The exact quote is: "Love anything, and your heart will certainly be wrung and possibly be broken. If you want to make sure of keeping it intact, you must give your heart to no one, not even to an animal." C.S. Lewis, *The Four Loves* (New York: Harcourt, Brace, 1960), 121.

Pastor and author John Piper gives the following six guidelines for loving each other amid differences:

- Let's avoid gossiping.

- Let's identify evidences of grace in each other and speak them to each other and about each other.

- Let's speak criticism directly to each other if we feel the need to speak to others about it.

- Let's look for, and assume, the best motive in the other's viewpoint, especially when we disagree.

- Let's think often of the magnificent things we hold in common.

- Let's be more amazed that we are forgiven than that we are right. And in that way, let's shape our relationships by the gospel.[3]

6. Look at the following list derived from Romans 12.

Love honestly, speaking out against what is wrong. (v. 9)
Love even unattractive people, because they are your brothers and sisters. (v. 10)
Love by making others feel honored and valuable. (v. 10)
Love by being generous in practical ways with your home, money, and time. (v. 13)
Love without bitterness. Don't "pay others back," or hold resentment against others. (v. 14)
Love with empathy. Be willing to be emotionally involved with others. (v. 15)
Love with humility. Be willing to associate with people who differ from you. (v. 16)

In which areas do you, as a group, tend to be the weakest, and why? What practical steps could you take to improve?

Discuss with your group.

[*The* Home Study *is a project. Read pages 78–79 in advance to help you prepare to lead your group through this project.*]

[*Pray for your group.*]

[3] Read the whole article for biblical support and explanation of these guidelines. John Piper, "Six Biblical Guidelines for Loving Each Other Amid Differences." *Desiring God: www.desiringgod.org/ResourceLibrary* (August 4, 2009)

Notes for Leaders

Session 5 Witness An Alternate City

[*Complete the* Home Study *on pages 80–82.*]

Bible Study Notes For Leaders

[*Read Acts 2:42–47 which describes the early church, and then work through the questions and notes below ahead of time to help you prepare to lead your group. The notes beneath the questions are not intended as answers to be read aloud. They are notes to help you facilitate the discussion.*]

1. What do we discover about how the early church learned together? What do we discover about fellowship and service? What can we learn from this?

The church trained and educated its members in community. "They devoted themselves to the apostles' teaching" (v. 42).

- "Devoted themselves" indicates a high commitment to learning.

- It was centered on the apostolic teaching. It was not learning in general, but rather the study of God's revelation as it came through the apostles. (Today, of course, the apostles' teaching is in the Bible.)

- Deeds of power accompanied and verified the truth of the apostles' preaching, as "many wonders and miraculous signs were done by the apostles" (v. 43). People were not simply taught what to believe, but given evidence for their belief. This point is missed unless we realize that verse 43 is not an isolated statement—it follows verse 42. The apostles' teaching (v. 42) was validated and verified by their miracles and wonders (v. 43). Hebrews 2:3–4 tells us that the purpose of miracles in the early church was to show listeners the truth of the gospel message brought by the apostles. A survey of the Bible reveals that miracles are not distributed randomly and evenly throughout history, but they generally come in clusters, for example when God sends a new set of messengers into the world. (Biblical revelation describes three general clusters of miracles—Moses and the Exodus; Elijah and the prophets before the exile; and Jesus and the apostles.) What's important to understand in verse 43 is that people were shown evidence of the truth of apostolic teaching, so they would devote themselves to it.

"They devoted themselves…to the fellowship" (v. 42). Fellowship and service didn't just happen; they worked at it.

- It was daily. "Every day" (v. 46), they were involved in each other's daily lives. They did not see each other only on Sundays, but the church brought its members together constantly.

- It was economic as well as "spiritual," for they "had everything in common" (v. 44). They recognized not only that other brothers and sisters had a claim on their time and their hearts, but also on their resources. People received practical, financial, and material help for their needs: "Selling their possessions and goods, they gave to anyone as he had need" (v. 45).

2. **The early church were so involved with each other that they had fellowship "every day." Do you have fellowship with another Christian every day? Is this possible? Why or why not?**

Discuss with your group.

3. What do we discover about how the early church worshiped and how they witnessed to others? What can we learn from this?

Worship had both an informal and formal aspect. It happened both in homes and in the temple courts. The church held both small group meetings ("they broke bread in their homes" in verse 46) and large group meetings ("continued to meet together in the temple courts" in verse 46).

- The church practiced the Lord's Supper, the "breaking of bread" (v. 42).

- There was a general spirit of joy ("glad and sincere hearts" in verse 46 and "praising God" in verse 47) which permeated their meetings.

- It was reverent as well as joyful. Notice that in the small group worship, the emphasis is on joy and gladness (v. 46), but in the large group, there is an emphasis on awe (v. 43).

- The church spent time in prayer, they "devoted themselves…to prayer" (v. 42).

Their witness to others was dynamic. The church was evangelistically effective with new conversions every day. "The Lord added…daily those who were being saved" (v. 47).

- It was based on a community life that was attractive to non-Christians. "Enjoying the favor of all the people" (v. 47) cannot mean that every non-Christian loved the early church, since there was plenty of persecution, but overall, the early church demonstrated the gospel in its community in a way that was irresistible to outside observers.

- It was church-centered. The person was "added to their number" (v. 47) and incorporated into the church.

4. British theologian Lesslie Newbigin observes:

> The gospel does not become public truth for a society by being propagated as a theory or as a worldview and certainly not as a religion. It can become public truth only insofar as it is embodied in a society (the church) which is both "abiding in" Christ and engaged in the life of the world.[1]

Do you agree with his assessment? Why or why not? Share examples.

Newbigin writes in *The Gospel in a Pluralistic Society*, "Those who call for a Christian assault on the worlds of politics and economics often make it clear...that the aim of the attack is to seize the levers of power and take control. We have seen many such successful revolutions, and we know that in most cases what has happened is simply that the oppressor and the oppressed have exchanged roles... The throne is unshaken, only there is a different person occupying it. How is the throne itself to be shaken?... Only by the power of the gospel itself, announced in word and embodied in deed... The victory of the Church over the demonic power which was embodied in the Roman imperial system was not won by seizing the levers of power: it was won when the victims knelt down in the Colosseum and prayed in the name of Jesus for the Emperor." [2]

| *Watch the DVD for Session 5 to help you prepare to lead your group through the discussion that follows.*

[1] Lesslie Newbigin, *Proper Confidence: Faith, Doubt and Certainty in Christian Discipleship* (Grand Rapids, Mich.: Eerdmans, 1995), 39.
[2] Lesslie Newbigin, *The Gospel in a Pluralistic Society* (Grand Rapids, Mich.: Eerdmans, 1989), 209–210.

Notes for Leaders

Discussion Questions Notes For Leaders

After watching the DVD with your group, use these questions to encourage discussion. The notes beneath the questions are not intended as answers to be read aloud. They are notes to help you facilitate the discussion.

You do not need to complete all the questions. Depending on the dynamic of the group and your time limit, you may find it helpful to choose in advance the questions that will be of most value to your group and start with those.

1. Was there anything from the DVD that was new to you, or had an effect on you? Did you hear anything that raised more questions in your mind?

Discuss with your group.

2. "An alternate city is gospel-speaking." What intimidates us about telling other people about Jesus? Are some people more intimidating than others? Why? What motivates us to tell people about Jesus?

The gospel produces a constellation of traits in us:

- First, we are compelled to share the gospel out of love.

- Second, we are freed from the fear of being ridiculed or hurt by others, since we already have the favor of God by grace.

- Third, there is a humility in our dealings with others, because we know we are saved only by grace, not because of our superior insight or character.

- Fourth, we are hopeful about anyone, even the "hard cases," because we were saved only because of grace ourselves.

- Fifth, we are courteous and careful with people. We don't have to push or coerce them, for it is God's grace that opens hearts, not our eloquence or persistence or even their openness.

If we are not effective in reaching others for Christ, it could be because of a lack of joy, a lack of humility and gentleness, or a lack of boldness.

- The joyful effects of the gospel in our own lives must give us an enormous energy for witness. How can we keep quiet about such a great wonder? If that energy is not there, we must repent and seek God until it flows.

- The humbling nature of the gospel must lead us to approach others without superiority. Since we are saved only by God's grace and not by our goodness, we expect to often find wisdom and compassion in others, which at many points may exceed our own. Are humility and respect present in us? If not, we will be ineffective.

- The love that we experience because of the gospel must remove from us the fear of others' disapproval. Is our boldness increasing? If not, we must repent and reflect on the gospel and God's acceptance of us until fear diminishes.

3. **"There is a credibility that comes if you are consistent in your behavior, there is a credibility that comes if people see the gospel transforming you." Do people notice your lifestyle and that of your community? Do they appreciate it, even if they don't understand it? Share examples.**

Discuss with your group.

4. **Frank Retief, a pastor and church planter in South Africa, writes, "people without Christ go to hell—if you really believe that you've got to take risks, take a chance and be prepared to fail."[3] What do you think of his statement?**

Discuss with your group. This question is intended to provoke discussion.

 [3] Bishop Frank Retief quoted in *Multiplying Churches,* edited by Stephen Timmis (Ross-shire, Scotland: Christian Focus Publications, 2000), 97.

5. A leading missiologist, C. Peter Wagner, writes, "Planting new churches is the most effective evangelistic methodology known under heaven."[4] Think of some reasons why starting new churches is a good way to reach people.

Often in new churches the sense of mission is strongest; more Christians have freedom to lead; and creative means of preaching the gospel are used. New churches, therefore, can best reach new generations, new residents, and new people groups.

Studies confirm that the average new congregation brings new people into the life of the body of Christ at many times the rate of an older congregation of the same size. In *Why Start New Churches?* Lyle Schaller reports, "The most important single argument for making new church development a high priority is this is the most effective means for reaching unchurched persons. Numerous studies have shown that 60 to 80 percent of the new adult members of new congregations are persons who were not actively involved in the life of any worshiping congregation immediately prior to joining that new mission. By contrast, most long established churches draw the majority of their new adult members from persons who transfer in from other congregations."[5]

Notice that many of the evangelistic challenges of the New Testament are calls to plant churches. The Great Commission (Matt. 28:18–20), for example, is a call not just to "make disciples" but to baptize. In Acts and elsewhere, it is clear that baptism means incorporation into a worshiping community with accountability and boundaries (see Acts 2:41–47).

Paul, the greatest missionary in history, had a rather simple twofold strategy. First, he went into the largest city of a region (see Acts 16:9, 12), and second, he planted churches in each town (Titus 1:5—"appoint elders in every town"). Once Paul had done that, he could say that he had "fully preached" the gospel in a region and that he had "no more place...to work in these regions" (Rom. 15:19, 23). This means Paul had two controlling assumptions: (a) that one of the best ways to influence a region was through its chief cities, and (b) that one of the best ways to influence a city was to plant churches in it. Once he had accomplished this, he moved on. He knew that the rest that needed to happen would follow.

[4] C. Peter Wagner, *Strategies for Church Growth* (Ventura, Calif.: Regal, 1987), 168–169. [5] Lyle Schaller, "Why Start New Churches?" in *The Circuit Rider*, May 1979, 3. Quoted in Donald Anderson McGavran and George G. Hunter III, *Church Growth: Strategies That Work* (Nashville: Abingdon, 1980), 100.

6. "When Christ returns to earth, the present age will end completely and the age to come will come fully. Meanwhile, we actually live between the two ages—in what's been called the overlap of the ages." What mistaken thoughts, distorted emotions, or wrong practices result when we don't focus enough on the age to come? What about when we don't focus enough on the present age?

John Stott in *The Contemporary Christian* suggests some applications:[6]

Personal change and growth

- The Holy Spirit has come into us already in the present age, subduing our fallen nature, our selfishness. So we have confidence that anyone can be changed, that any enslaving habit can be overcome.

- On the other hand, our fallen nature remains in us and will never be eliminated until the age to come. We must avoid pat answers, and we must not expect "quick fixes." We must be patient and understanding with growing persons and not condescending or impatient toward lapses and failures.

Church change and growth

- The church is now the community of kingdom power. Since Christ is ruling over the present age we can be confident that God can bring church revival and transformation.

- On the other hand, error and evil will never be completely eradicated from the church until the age to come. We must not be harshly critical of imperfect congregations, nor jump impatiently from church to church over perceived blemishes.

Social change

- Since Christ is ruling over the present age we can expect to use God's power to change social conditions and communities.

- On the other hand, until the age to come there will be "wars and rumors of wars." Selfishness, cruelty, terrorism, and oppression will continue. Christians harbor no illusions about politics nor expect utopian conditions. The age to come means that Christians will not trust any political or social agenda to bring about righteousness here on earth.

[6] Adapted from the chapter "The Now and the Not Yet," John Stott, *The Contemporary Christian* (Downers Grove, Ill.: IVP, 1992).

A few more examples follow:

When we don't focus on the age to come, we may give preeminence to other objects

Other things—perhaps very good things—become too important to us. We can easily make family or work or even our moral record more important than God in our life. When we look to them for more joy and hope than we do to God, they become central to our life and we get distortions.

When we don't focus on the present age, we may forget the importance of unity

In John 17, Jesus directly links Christian oneness to the manifestation of God to the world. The implication is that visible unity is an important way to show the world the glory of God.

When we don't focus on the present age, we may forget the importance of social justice

If the purpose of the kingdom of God is to heal all the results of sin—spiritual, psychological, social and physical—then we must also intentionally use our gifts and resources to fight disintegration in every area.

When we don't focus on the present age, we may forget the importance of witness

2 Corinthians 5:19–20 says, "God was reconciling the world to himself in Christ, not counting men's sins against them. And he has committed to us the message of reconciliation. We are therefore Christ's ambassadors, as though God were making his appeal through us." It is an amazing description of our purpose in this present age—we are Christ's ambassadors.

[*Pray for your group.*]

Notes for Leaders

Session 6 Work Cultivating The Garden

[*Complete the* Home Study *on pages 88–98.*]

Bible Study Notes For Leaders

[*Read Matthew 6:19–21 and then work through the questions and notes below ahead of time to help you prepare to lead your group. The notes beneath the questions are not intended as answers to be read aloud. They are notes to help you facilitate the discussion.*]

1. Why does Jesus tell us to store up "treasures in heaven" (v. 20) rather than "treasures on earth" (v. 19)? What does Jesus mean when he says, "For where your treasure is, there your heart will be also"?

Literally Jesus is saying not to treasure earthly treasures, but to treasure heavenly treasure. Everybody, at the center of his or her soul, treasures something. To treasure something means to look at it and fill your heart with the beauty and the value of it.

Whatever that treasure is—if it is not God—it will enslave you. You will pay any price for it. You will do anything to get it. An inordinate dependence on money or material things, for example, has the peculiar effect of blinding you spiritually. Moreover, earthly treasures don't actually give you the security and significance they seem to promise. They can't possibly stop all the things—death, tragedy, broken relationships—that come along.

You give to what you treasure. You always give most effortlessly to whatever is your real salvation, your hope, your meaning in life. If your real hope is in your appearance, career, status, or comfort, your giving will flow more easily into those items and symbols. If Jesus is your real hope, your giving flows out easily into his work and the lives of people.

Jesus is asking, "Are you willing to lose it all for me? Are you willing to let me have complete control of your life? Are you willing to make me the new source of your meaning and your identity and your security? Am I your treasure?"

2. How do most people you know tend to spend their time, energy, and money? What do you spend money on most effortlessly and joyfully?

Money is one of the best ways to identify the idols of our heart. Even if money is not an idol, money will often show us where our idols are. We can find out what our heart most loves and adores and worships and rests in for salvation—often it is where we most effortlessly and easily and joyfully spend money.

It may be useful to give this exercise to your group if the members have never done anything similar.

- Estimate what percentage of your money is currently going to the following.

    1. Christian ministry—church, Christian workers, other ministries.
    2. People outside your family with economic needs.

- Think about what this percentage says about your heart and treasure.

- Decide what percentage of your income you will give this year. Make it a sacrificial level. Identify in your own mind the sacrifices that you will have to make.

- Prayerfully determine how to distribute your giving among causes you feel will honor God.

- Decide at what intervals you will give, and plan a way to keep a record of how well you follow your plan.

3. How might you and your group go about storing up "treasures in heaven"?

Examples include:

- Giving money and possessions away in sacrificial proportions with joy.

- Giving that entails sacrifices in our daily lifestyle—how much we spend on clothes, travel, home, and so on.

- Giving radically to others rather than accruing surplus wealth to guarantee a financially secure future.

- Always looking for opportunities to help among our friends, our neighbors, the poor, in our church, in our city.

- Remembering that God is the owner of all things, and we are just the stewards of his wealth.

- Using our resources not for personal ends but for the protection of those with less.

- Taking genuine care of the widows, the poor, and the immigrants—the powerless.

- Modeling to the world a redeemed society in which wealth and possessions are used to build up community and not for personal fulfillment.

- Choosing, thinking about, and working at our jobs in a way that honors God, not as a way of accruing personal wealth, status, comfort, and so on.

4. One way to ensure that we store up treasures in heaven is to celebrate, reflect on, and give thanks for our treasures on earth. This is part of what we do on the Sabbath. In an article called "Bring Back the Sabbath" in *The New York Times Magazine* we read,

> There is ample evidence that our relationship to work is out of whack. Let me argue on behalf of an institution that has kept workaholism in reasonable check for thousands of years. Most people mistakenly believe that all you have to do to stop working is not work. The inventors of the Sabbath understood that it was a much more complicated undertaking. You cannot downshift casually and easily. This is why the Puritan and Jewish Sabbaths were so exactingly intentional. The rules did not exist to torture the faithful. Interrupting the ceaseless round of striving requires a surprisingly strenuous act of will, one that has to be bolstered by habit as well as by social sanction.[1]

This quote explains that scheduled rest will not work without a great deal of intentionality and discipline. Brainstorm the kind of practical habits and useful practices that can help us observe Sabbath.

Determine what to do with the time

• Take time for contemplative rest.

Prayer and worship is a critical part of Sabbath, from any perspective. It is the basis for "inner rest," and provides respite from the more exhausting exertions of life.

• Take time for recreational rest.

The Puritans and others were skeptical of recreations that required a great deal of money and time and exertion. Be careful to ensure that recreation really refreshes.

• Take time for aesthetic rest.

We need to expose ourselves to works of God's creation that refresh and energize us and that we find beautiful. This may mean outdoor experiences. This may also mean the arts—music, drama, visual art, and so on.

• Take some sheer inactivity time.

Almost all of us need some time every week that is unplanned and unstructured, so we can do whatever we spontaneously feel like doing. If our Sabbath time is simply a very

[1] J. Shulevitz, "Bring Back the Sabbath" *New York Times Magazine* (March 2, 2003).

busy time filled with scheduled activities of recreation and ministry, it will not suffice. There must be some "cessation" from exertion.

Honor both macro- and micro-rhythms and seasons in your rest

Israel's Sabbath cycles of rest-and-work included not only Sabbath days but Sabbath years and even a Jubilee, the seventh Sabbath year. This is an important insight for workers in today's world.

It is possible to voluntarily take on an insufficient-Sabbath-time season of work. For example, if you want to be a doctor, you are going to have to be a resident. Many other jobs demand an initial investment of time with a heavy work week. Also, going into business for yourself or undertaking a major project may require something similar. We can enter a season like this for a time, but we need to be accountable to someone for this or we will get locked into an "under-Sabbathed" lifestyle. During the "under-Sabbathed" time, we must not let rhythms of prayer, Bible study, and worship die.

Inject Sabbath into the rest of the work week

If you develop the "inner rest" of Sabbath, it will lead you to be less frantic and driven in the rest of your work.

Associated with the Sabbath laws were the gleaning laws. According to these laws, the owners of fields were not allowed to harvest out to the edges of their fields. They left a percentage of grain in the field for the poor to come and take. Sabbath, then, is the deliberate limitation of productivity, as a way to trust God and be a good steward of yourself and your resources.

In our case this may mean deliberately setting fewer goals for ourselves in a given day and week, not "harvesting out to the edges." The purpose of Sabbath is not simply to rejuvenate yourself in order to do more work. Nor is it the pursuit of pleasure. The purpose of Sabbath is to enjoy God, life in general, what you have accomplished in the world through his help, and the freedom you have in the gospel—the freedom from slavery to any material object or human expectation. The Sabbath is a sign of the whole future salvation that is coming.

Watch the DVD for Session 6 to help you prepare to lead your group through the discussion that follows.

Discussion Questions Notes For Leaders

After watching the DVD with your group, use these questions to encourage discussion. The notes beneath the questions are not intended as answers to be read aloud. They are notes to help you facilitate the discussion.

You do not need to complete all the questions. Depending on the dynamic of the group and your time limit, you may find it helpful to choose in advance the questions that will be of most value to your group and start with those.

1. Was there anything from the DVD that was new to you, or had an effect on you? Did you hear anything that raised more questions in your mind?

Discuss with your group.

2. What are some of the practical implications of the biblical teachings that work is good and has dignity?

The ancient Greeks saw the material world (and therefore manual labor, or work-for-pay) as demeaning and degrading. A work-free, contemplative life was considered the most humanizing, ennobling, and ideal life. Work was seen as an unmixed burden and curse.

Unfortunately, a strong strain of this thinking has come down to us and created a hierarchy for our work, from the "nobler" work of the philosopher down through the helping professions and on down to manual labor. Today, people often find their dignity or identity in doing work that is high-status and high-paying. Many people take jobs that they don't like and/or aren't good at, simply because they are higher-status jobs. This thinking has even invaded the church. In many churches it is either implicitly or explicitly stated that full-time ministry is the way to really please God, while all other jobs are just "secular work."

The biblical view of the dignity of all work puts an end to this type of thinking. Work matters to God.

3. What are some of the practical implications of the biblical teachings that we must not separate God from our work?

Christianity is not simply a set of beliefs to be held in order to save my individual soul. It is also an interpretation of (and a distinct way of understanding) everything in the world. It brings a distinct perspective on human nature, right and wrong, justice, beauty, and character. If you believe the universe happened by accident—as opposed to being created by a loving, redeeming God—then you will have to have a different view of every one of these fundamental issues. And these issues determine how you live your daily life, and how you do and think about your work.

The fact is that all work must be done out of some worldview. For example, if you believe that this world is all there is, and therefore all moral values are relative and there is no afterlife, this understanding will have an effect on how you do your work.

The problem comes for Christians when they enter a work-world that is operating according to different worldviews. The temptation for Christians is to simply plunge into workplaces dominated by these worldviews and conduct their working lives in accordance with the reigning paradigms, rather than thinking out the implications of the gospel for how they can do their work with Christian distinctiveness.

The Bible tells us that Jesus has to be Lord of every area of life, not just of our private lives. The gospel should shape and affect the motives, manner, and methods with which we carry out every task in life, including our work. God matters to our work.

4. Besides telling coworkers about Christ, what does it mean to "bring the gospel into your work"? Brainstorm some ways that you can work with Christian distinctiveness in your workplace.

To be a Christian in your workplace means much more than just being honest, or not sleeping with your coworkers. It even means more than personal witnessing and holding a Bible study at your place of work. Rather, it means thinking out the implications of the gospel and God's kingship for your entire work-life.

Below is just one list of possible implications and applications. As Christians we will be:

- Working with more job satisfaction, because our job is not an idol.

- Exhibiting honesty and integrity in our work, and not cutting corners to benefit ourselves at the expense of other employees, customers, or the community.

- Listening, building community, being welcoming, being humble in our workplace.

- Working with a commitment to delayed gratification, and showing self-control and discipline in our work. We will be looking to long-term benefits for all, not just short-term benefits for ourselves.

- Seeking jobs that promote the common good and are congruent with our gifts, not just to make money.

- Displaying attitudes toward economic justice. We will not be assessing persons in pure economic terms or paying people as little as the market will bear. Our desire will be to promote the general welfare of workers, so they flourish not only professionally but personally.

- Being honest in advertising and promotion. This is not only honesty in presenting ourselves, but seeking to cater to the best desires in customers, not the worst.

- Producing products that benefit people and communities. Our desire will be to help the company's broader community and neighborhood flourish.

- Neither overworking nor underworking.

5. In Matthew 11, Jesus promises to "give us rest" (v. 28). How can the deep rest Jesus gives us in the gospel change our relationship to our work?

To get a deeper picture of what happens to our work in Christ, look at Matthew 11:28–30. When Jesus calls all people to himself, he says that he knows we are "weary and burdened," and that we need "rest" (v. 28). In verse 30 he offers his cure: a "burden" and even a "yoke"! This was, of course, the harness put on a beast of burden, so it was a symbol of slavery, grinding work, and toil. How could a yoke be a solution to the problem of deep weariness?

Jesus says that it is *his* yoke and *his* burden—that these are the only yoke and burden that are "light." Why? "For I am gentle and humble in heart, and you will find rest for your souls" (v. 29).

Jesus directly claims that he is the only "boss" who will not drive you into the ground. Only when we have an identity, meaning, and significance based in Jesus—something beyond our work—will we find deep rest for our souls, a rest that will abide with us in our work. Why? Only Jesus offers us a finished work to rest in. Remember, a Christian is not just someone who admires Jesus, emulates Jesus, or obeys Jesus. A Christian is someone who rests in Jesus' finished work instead of his or her own.

We must have this deep spiritual rest, or else we will experience a weariness that vacations can't cure. You won't be able to relax, even when you are supposed to be resting. Many people put enormous pressure on work to be satisfying, profitable, and fulfilling. Only if we get the deep rest of the gospel will we be able to live a life happily in the 99 percent of the world's jobs that are neither very fulfilling nor very lucrative.

Learn to see the signs of a deeper weariness that time off and vacation are not healing. Ask yourself these questions:

- Am I making work too important—an idol?
- Am I making money, status, or control (as a means to freedom, leisure/pleasure, or just significance) too important—an idol?
- Am I doing work that I am not gifted/able to do? Why did I take this job?
- Are sins in others (such as greed, pride, bitterness, fear) making this particular work environment crushing and probably not fixable? Do I need a new job?

6. **"Do you see your workplace as a place to share the gospel as well as a place to let the gospel shape how you work"? What can you bring into your profession that is uniquely helpful?**

Discuss with your group.

[*The* Home Study *is a project. Read pages 104–105 in advance to help you prepare to lead your group through this project.*]

[*Pray for your group.*]

Notes for Leaders

Session 7 Justice A People For Others

[*Complete the* Home Study *on pages 106–116.*]

[*Complete the* Home Study *on pages 106–116.*]

Bible Study Notes For Leaders

[*Read Luke 10:25–37 and then work through the questions and notes below ahead of time to help you prepare to lead your group. The notes beneath the questions are not intended as answers to be read aloud. They are notes to help you facilitate the discussion.*]

1. On the basis of Jesus' teaching, who is our neighbor?

In effect, the law expert was saying to Jesus, "Come on, now. Be reasonable! You don't mean we have to love everyone like this, do you? Who is my neighbor?"

Jesus responded by making a Samaritan and a Jew the two main characters in his parable. They were extreme enemies, yet the Samaritan gave aid in spite of the following facts:

- It was extremely dangerous for the Samaritan to stop on a desolate road infested with robbers.

- It was very expensive for the Samaritan to give the innkeeper a promise to pay whatever it might cost to care for the man until he recovered.

Jesus' answer is clear and devastating; it demolishes any limitations put on our mercy. We are to help people of other races and religions, even from groups we have a historical reason to distrust. We are to help, even when it is risky and costly to us.

In summary, we are to love in word and deed anyone we find in need, anyone we find in the road. They are our neighbors.

2. Shouldn't we help members of our own family and of our own Christian community first?

It is certainly natural that our involvement would be much deeper with family and usually with other Christians in our community (Gal. 6:10), but Jesus forbids us from being exclusive. The parable shows a priest and a Levite trying to get to the other side of the road from the needy man. They avoid walking directly over him physically, but obviously they are guilty of neglect, because he is in their road, even though they try to create the illusion that he is not. In the same way, everyone else where we live is "in our road." If we don't learn about or get involved in any way with the needs of others, we are like the priest and the Levite in the parable.

3. How does Jesus illustrate what the true motive should be for showing mercy to our neighbor?

Remember, Jesus told this story to a Jewish man, so it was a remarkable twist when he put the Jewish man in the parable.

What if the parable had gone like this? "A Samaritan was beaten up and left half dead in a road. A man came along and saw him and had compassion and ministered to him." The hearer would have said, "How ridiculous! I would never do such a thing! Samaritans hate us and we hate them. They are enemies."

Instead, Jesus put the hearer in the road as the victim, so the parable goes like this: "Imagine if *you* were beaten up and left half dead on the road. What if your only hope was to get help from someone who not only did not owe you any help but who actually owed you the opposite. What if your only hope was to get free grace from someone who had every reason to trample you?"

Notice, when Jesus asked who the neighbor was, the law expert admitted it was the "one who had mercy on him" (vv. 36–37). The man realized that, of course, he would want mercy from even an enemy.

Jesus then said to him, "Go and do likewise" (v. 37). Jesus is saying, "If you see that you have been saved by grace, then your attitude toward others will be one of compassion." If you see that you have been saved graciously by someone who owes you the opposite, then you will show grace to others.

4. **The following quotes are cited by Rodney Stark, a historian and sociologist who studied the reasons why Christianity spread in the Roman Empire. The Greco-Roman world was struck by several huge plagues or epidemics. Stark traces how the Christians' reaction to the plagues differed dramatically from that of those who maintained faith in traditional, polytheistic paganism.**

> The impious Galileans [Christians] support not only their poor, but ours as well, everyone can see that our people lack aid from us.
>
> Roman Emperor Julian (around 360 AD)[1]

> [During the great epidemic] most of our brother Christians showed unbounded love and loyalty, never sparing themselves... Heedless of danger, they took charge of the sick, attending to their every need and ministering to them in Christ... Many, in nursing and curing others, transferred their death to themselves and died in their stead... The [pagans] behaved in the very opposite way. At the first onset of the disease, they pushed the sufferers away and fled even from their dearest, throwing them into the roads before they were dead.
>
> Dionysius, Bishop of Alexandria (around 260 AD)[2]

Having read these quotes, what is the effect of unselfish service on others? Have you found this to be true in your own experience? Give examples.

In this particular case, because Christians had a strong assurance of salvation and a pattern of self-giving service in Christ's sacrifice on the cross, they did not abandon the sick or flee the cities but cared for the sick, both Christian and pagan. Many of the survivors owed their lives to the Christian church. The esteem of the church in the culture in general increased, and people listened to the gospel message as a result.

The gospel is the good news that we are forgiven by God's grace, and that the whole world will one day be renewed by God's grace. That is why deeds that alleviate suffering are so integral to the declaration of the gospel. In one sense, showing mercy to our neighbor is a result of the gospel, because as converted people we live like the one who saved us. In another sense, showing mercy to our neighbor is itself a gospel proclamation. It preaches the gospel through our actions.

> *Watch the DVD for Session 7 to help you prepare to lead your group through the discussion that follows.*

[1] Quoted in Rodney Stark, *The Rise of Christianity* (San Francisco: Harper, 1997), 84. [2] Ibid., 82–83.

Discussion Questions Notes For Leaders

After watching the DVD with your group, use these questions to encourage discussion. The notes beneath the questions are not intended as answers to be read aloud. They are notes to help you facilitate the discussion.

You do not need to complete all the questions. Depending on the dynamic of the group and your time limit, you may find it helpful to choose in advance the questions that will be of most value to your group and start with those.

1. Was there anything from the DVD that was new to you, or had an effect on you? Did you hear anything that raised more questions in your mind?

Discuss with your group.

2. "*Shalom* means total flourishing in absolutely every dimension: physically, relationally, socially, and spiritually." In what practical ways can you and your group "resolve to have shalom felt everywhere…and begin to reweave the broken fabric of creation"? What can you as a group (or a church) bring into your neighborhood that is uniquely helpful?

The fabric of creation has been eaten away by sin in every aspect. Because of sin, our bodies, our relationships, and our societies are always breaking down and pulling apart rather than cohering in harmony and unity. For example:

Slavery to personal idols

- Anything more important than Christ for happiness (e.g., career or family) becomes our master.
- Shalom means allowing Jesus, as Savior and Lord, to liberate us from the power of false masters (e.g., from overwork, excessive anxiety over children, and so on.)

Slavery to cultural idols

- Every field of human endeavor puts forth something other than God—financial profit, individual rights or happiness, human reason, group power—as the ultimate value and goal.

- Shalom means doing our work with kingdom values, so it will be distinctive.

Slavery to social idols

- The world attaches high value to power, comfort, success, and recognition.

- God's kingdom is won not through strength and accomplishment, however, but through the cross. It is entered not by the strong, but by those who admit their weakness and need for grace. This completely changes our attitude toward the poor, the powerless, and the marginal. Shalom means working toward peace and social justice.

3. Benjamin Fernando from Sri Lanka writes,

There is no such thing as a separate individual gospel and a separate social gospel. There is only one gospel—a redeemed man in a reformed society... Social problems assume greater importance in Christianity than in Buddhism or Hinduism. The theory of Karma and rebirth gives a fairly reasonable explanation for social inequalities of this life which on the one hand are consequences of the previous life and on the other hand can be compensated for in the next life. But to a Christian there is only one earthly life and so social problems have to be dealt with now or never.[3]

Do you agree with his assessment that "social problems have to be dealt with now or never"? Why or why not?

Discuss with your group. This question is intended to provoke discussion.

[3] Benjamin E. Fernando, "The Evangel and Social Upheaval (part 2)", in *Christ Seeks Asia*, ed. W.S. Mooneyham (Charlestown, Ind.: Rock House, 1969), 118–119.

4. **The Bible reveals at least three causal factors for poverty: injustice and oppression; circumstantial calamity; and personal failure. Do you agree? Can you give examples of these from the Bible or from your own experience?**

The biblical Wisdom Literature provides a remarkably balanced and nuanced view of the root causes of poverty.

- Injustice and oppression: This refers to any unjust social condition or treatment that keeps a person in poverty. Examples include social systems weighted in favor of the powerful (Lev. 19:15), high-interest loans (Ex. 22:25–27).

- Circumstantial calamity: This refers to any natural disaster or circumstance that brings or keeps a person in poverty. The Bible is filled with examples, such as the famine in Genesis 47.

- Personal failure: Poverty can also be caused by one's own personal sins and failures, such as indolence (Prov. 6:6–11) and other problems with self-discipline (Prov. 23:21).

These three factors are often intertwined. They do not usually produce separate categories of poverty except in acute situations, such as a hurricane that leaves people homeless and in need of immediate, short-term, material care. Rather, the three factors are usually interactively present.

On the one hand, the Bible strongly endorses hard work and frugality—qualities that virtually always lead to some degree of prosperity. Also, it promotes and recognizes the place of private ownership of property and provides many safeguards against theft.

On the other hand, the Bible strongly promotes relative economic equality in society. Hard work does not necessarily lead to material prosperity. Relative equality is sought partly through individual generosity, but not exclusively. The gleaning laws and the Sabbath and Jubilee years were social structures that limited profit-taking and income production.

The Old Testament is full of prophetic denunciations against social injustice to the poor. Amos 5:11–12 says, "You trample on the poor and force him to give you grain. Therefore, though you have built stone mansions, you will not live in them; though you have planted lush vineyards, you will not drink their wine. For I know how many are your offenses and how great your sins. You oppress the righteous and take bribes and you deprive the poor of justice in the courts." Ezekiel 22:29 says, "The people of the land practice extortion and commit robbery; they oppress the poor and needy and mistreat the alien, denying them justice."

Unlike many ancient cultures and some modern philosophies, the Bible does not see being poor as a curse from God; yet poverty and material deprivation are in no way glamorized, seen as an intrinsic good, or considered something to simply be accepted. Unlike many ancient cultures and some modern philosophies, the Bible does not see being wealthy as necessarily a blessing from God. It can be an enormous spiritual trap; yet rich people are in no way demonized or seen as intrinsically oppressive. No one is saved or blessed simply because of being materially poor, nor is anyone condemned simply because of being materially rich.

5. **"It's natural to want to help people who are like you, who like you, and who you like." What would it mean for you, specifically, to help people who are not like you, who do not like you, and who you do not like?**

God tells Israel, "The alien living with you must be treated as one of your native-born. Love him as yourself, for you were aliens in Egypt. I am the LORD your God" (Lev. 19:34). The Israelites had been "aliens" and oppressed slaves in Egypt, without the ability to free themselves—God liberated them by his grace and power. Now they are to treat all people who have less power or fewer assets than they do as their neighbors, doing love, justice, and mercy to them. The basis for "doing justice," then, is salvation by grace. Christians may disagree about the particular political approach to the problems of injustice and poverty, but all Christians must be characterized by their passion for justice, and by their personal commitment to ameliorate injustice through personal giving, sacrifice, and generosity.

6. Jonathan Edwards once was preaching on how important it was to give to the poor. Someone later objected, "I can't afford to give to the poor." Edwards responded with an application of Galatians 6:2.

> In many cases, we may, by the rules of the gospel, be obliged to give to others, when we cannot do it without suffering ourselves... If our neighbor's difficulties and necessities be much greater than our own, and we see that he is not like to be otherwise relieved, we should be willing to suffer with him, and to take part of his burden on ourselves; else how is that rule of bearing one another's burdens fulfilled? If we are never obliged to relieve others' burdens, but when we can do it without burdening ourselves, then how do we bear our neighbor's burdens, when we bear no burden at all?[4]

Do you agree that we are not only to help others with our excess time, money, and emotional resources, but that we are to give until it burdens us? What will this mean for you and your group?

Only when we give until it burdens us are we truly bearing one another's burdens. Discuss what it means in your context to help not only with your excess time, money, and emotional resources, but until it burdens you. Be practical.

[*Pray for your group.*]

[4] Jonathan Edwards, *The Works of Jonathan Edwards* (Edinburgh: Banner of Truth, 1834), Volume 2, 171.

Notes for Leaders

Session 8 Eternity The World That Is To Come

[*Complete the* Home Study *on pages 124–139.*]

Bible Study Notes For Leaders

[*Read Isaiah 60:15–22 and then work through the questions and notes below ahead of time to help you prepare to lead your group. The notes beneath the questions are not intended as answers to be read aloud. They are notes to help you facilitate the discussion.*]

1. **What will heaven be like according to Isaiah's description in verses 17–21? How does this compare with the description in Revelation 21:1–4, 22–27?**

   - v. 17 The city will be made of metal—gold, silver, bronze, and iron—which implies security and stability. In Revelation the city is described as being made of precious gems (Rev. 21:18–21) which also implies permanence.

   - vv. 17–18 There will be peace and righteousness. There will be no violence or ruin or destruction. Revelation 21:4 takes up this theme also.

   - vv. 19–20 The sun and moon will not be necessary because God's presence in the city is all the light needed. This is also what is described in Revelation 21:23.

2. **How can the knowledge that there will be no violence or destruction in the future kingdom help us, and those we come into contact with, to cope with the violence and destruction we experience around us?**

   Discuss with your group.

3. **God is described in a variety of ways and given a variety of titles in this passage. What do we learn about God and what does it mean for our relationship with him?**

- v. 16 "the Lord"

- v. 16 "your Savior"

- v. 16 "your Redeemer"

- v. 16 "the Mighty One of Jacob"

- v. 19 "your everlasting light"

- v. 19 "your God will be your glory"

This is a good time to review some of the things you have learned about God through this course.

In his commentary on this passage of Isaiah, John Oswalt writes: "Throughout Israel's history, God's purpose was that Israel should know him. This is one of the most moving notes in biblical theology: the transcendent Creator, the only self-existent Being in the universe, wants his creatures to know him. Why? Because only through the knowledge of him is there any hope of our reaching the possibilities for which we were created. Thus in the Exodus God says that it is all in order that they may know him. Thus it was also in the establishment of Israel in the promised land, in the return from exile, in the coming of the Messiah, and now here in the culmination of all things at the end of the age. What is it that God's activity on behalf of his people will teach? That he is the Savior, the Redeemer! All creation shouts of its Creator, of his beauty, his order, his power, and his truth. But what of God when his creatures have corrupted their way and turned his beauty to ugliness, his order to chaos, his power to oppression, and his truth to lies? Will he abandon us to our well-deserved fates? No, he will not. God is not only the Creator—he is the Savior... God, the Mighty One of Jacob...reaches out to us and offers us the means in the Servant-Messiah of transcending sin, failure, guilt, and shame."[1]

[1] John N. Oswalt, *The Book of Isaiah Chapters 40–66*, The New International Commentary on the Old Testament (Grand Rapids, Mich.: Eerdmans, 1998), 553.

4. Richard Mouw writes:

> My own hunch is that God has provided us with a rich storehouse of diverse images of the afterlife, all of them hints in the direction of something that is beyond our present comprehension, so that we can be free to draw on one or another of them as a particular situation in our life may require.[2]

In what situations might we draw on the description of heaven in Isaiah 60? What other descriptions of eternity have you drawn on in the past and why?

Discuss with your group.

Read Isaiah 60:1–14 and watch the DVD for Session 8 to help you prepare to lead your group through the discussion that follows.

[2] Richard J. Mouw, *When the Kings Come Marching In* (Grand Rapids, Mich.: Eerdmans, 2002), x.

Session 8 Eternity The World That Is To Come

Discussion Questions Notes For Leaders

After watching the DVD with your group, use these questions to encourage discussion. The notes beneath the questions are not intended as answers to be read aloud. They are notes to help you facilitate the discussion.

You do not need to complete all the questions. Depending on the dynamic of the group and your time limit, you may find it helpful to choose in advance the questions that will be of most value to your group and start with those.

1. Was there anything from the DVD that was new to you, or had an effect on you? Did you hear anything that raised more questions in your mind?

Discuss with your group.

2. Isaiah 60 describes a vision of the New Jerusalem as incorporating the cultural achievements of all people and all nations. What aspects of your work do you think might be incorporated into this final kingdom? How does this affect your understanding of your work?

This question will be easier to answer for some industries, for example, health care/ medicine, law/justice, education, the arts, and other service-oriented industries. People may find more difficulty answering for fields including finance, advertising, entertainment, etc.

However, when we recognize that the vision of the New Jerusalem includes the full-orbed idea of human flourishing, we can see that economic growth and wealth are part of this vision. Similarly, advertising and entertainment integrate beauty, longing, and joy with what we call "popular culture." These things will be enjoyed as an appropriate way to honor the work of God's new creation (and all the human cultural achievements integrated therein).

3. **The community described here is one of perfectly restored shalom. What are some tangible ways that the church can be a better foretaste of that community?**

Examples include justice and mercy ministries, radical commitment to reconciliation with one another, forgiveness, unity, sharing of wealth and power, fighting disease and hunger and providing help for the sick and physically afflicted, doing our jobs with excellence, with integrity, with love, and with an eye to helping others around us, etc.

This is a chance to review all that has been learned in the last seven sessions.

4. **What are some things that are competing with God as your "glory" and your "everlasting light"? What do you think would change if God were your only glory and everlasting light?**

Discuss with your group.

5. **Now that you have completed the gospelⁱⁿlife course, take a few minutes to look back through your notes and then share with the group one thing that changed or affected you, and explain why. Pray about these discoveries and realizations during your time of prayer together.**

Write down people's answers so that you can pray about them. Encourage your group to do the same.

[*Pray for your group.*]

Assessment

> *Once you have completed Session 8, schedule a time to meet individually with your group members to discuss their next steps and to pray with them about their plans.*

> *When you meet, review their gospel self-assessment questionnaire—they should have completed it during their* Home Study *for Session 8. See pages 134–139 of this guide.*

> *Ask them how their understanding of the gospel has progressed during the course.*

For example, ask them to comment on:

- their understanding of grace and their new identity in Christ
- the nature and dynamic of sin and idolatry in a Christian's life
- why Christians are called to live in community
- what it means to submit to God's view of money, sex, and power
- ways to reflect an eternal perspective through how we use our time, energy, money, and resources at home, in the workplace, and in the world.

> *Help them come up with some concrete and practical plans that put into practice the things learned during this course.*

For example, encourage them to:

- remember to repent not only of their sins, but also of their "so-called" righteousness
- pray regularly about identifying and dismantling the idols in their life
- find people who can hold them accountable for what they have learned in the course
- sign up for another course, or put together a reading list to help continue their "progress and joy in the faith" (Phil. 1:25)

- join a group (if they haven't already) that meets regularly to spend time together, study the Bible, and pray

- pray about which of the community-building practices they need to apply better, and then do it

- get involved in some form of service at church on Sundays

- think of ways to continually invite their non-Christian friends and colleagues to church or church events

- think about how they can support church planting

- think about the city and how they can love and serve the city

- get involved in some form of justice or mercy ministry

- think "worldviewishly" about their work by asking the questions on page 97 and by encouraging other Christians to join in the debate. Help them to think especially about the immediate opportunities in their workplace for (a) serving people, (b) serving society, and (c) witnessing to Christ.

[*Write down the next steps, and then pray together about them.*]

Share Your Thoughts

With the Author: Your comments will be forwarded to the author when you send them to *zauthor@zondervan.com*.

With Zondervan: Submit your review of this book by writing to *zreview@zondervan.com*.

Free Online Resources at
www.zondervan.com

Zondervan AuthorTracker: Be notified whenever your favorite authors publish new books, go on tour, or post an update about what's happening in their lives at www.zondervan.com/ authortracker.

Daily Bible Verses and Devotions: Enrich your life with daily Bible verses or devotions that help you start every morning focused on God. Visit www.zondervan.com/newsletters.

Free Email Publications: Sign up for newsletters on Christian living, academic resources, church ministry, fiction, children's resources, and more. Visit www.zondervan.com/newsletters.

Zondervan Bible Search: Find and compare Bible passages in a variety of translations at www.zondervanbiblesearch.com.

Other Benefits: Register yourself to receive online benefits like coupons and special offers, or to participate in research.

ZONDERVAN®

ZONDERVAN.com/
AUTHORTRACKER
follow your favorite authors

TWO SONS, ONE WHO KEPT THE RULES RELIGIOUSLY AND ONE WHO BROKE THEM ALL. ONE FATHER WHO LOVED BOTH LOST SONS BEYOND ANYTHING THEY COULD IMAGINE.

The Prodigal God curriculum kit contains everything that your church needs to experience a six-week preaching and small group campaign.

In this compelling film and study, pastor and *New York Times* bestselling author Timothy Keller opens your eyes to the powerful message of Jesus' best-known—and least understood—parable: The Parable of the Prodigal Son.

Dr. Keller helps you and your small group or church glean insights from each of the characters in Jesus' parable; the irreligious younger son, the moralistic elder son, and the father who lavishes love on both.

SESSION TITLES:

1. The Parable
2. The People Around Jesus
3. The Two Lost Sons
4. The Elder Brother
5. The True Elder Brother
6. The Feast of the Father

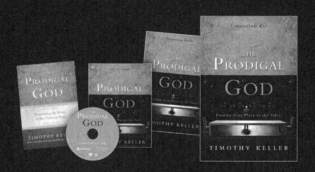

Session one contains the full 38-minute film. Each of the other five sessions will feature a short (2-3 minute) recap segment from the full length film to set up the small group discussion.

THE KIT CONTAINS ONE OF EACH OF THE FOLLOWING:

The Prodigal God DVD, *The Prodigal God* Discussion Guide, *The Prodigal God* hardcover book, and "Getting Started Guide." *Mixed Media Set 978-0-310-32075-3*

ALSO AVAILABLE:

Discussion Guide *(purchase one for each group member)* 978-0-310-32536-9

DVD *(purchase one for each group)* 978-0-310-32535-2

Hardcover book *(available in case lots of 24 only)* 978-0-310-32697-7

PICK UP A COPY AT YOUR FAVORITE BOOKSTORE!

 ZONDERVAN® .com   www.theprodigalgod.com    REDEEMER CITY to CITY